*TWAYNE'S WORLD AUTHORS SERIES*

*A Survey of the World's Literature*

Sylvia E. Bowman, Indiana University

GENERAL EDITOR

# SPAIN

Janet W. Diaz, University of North Carolina, Chapel Hill

Gerald E. Wade, Vanderbilt University

EDITORS

Fernando de Rojas

*TWAS 368*

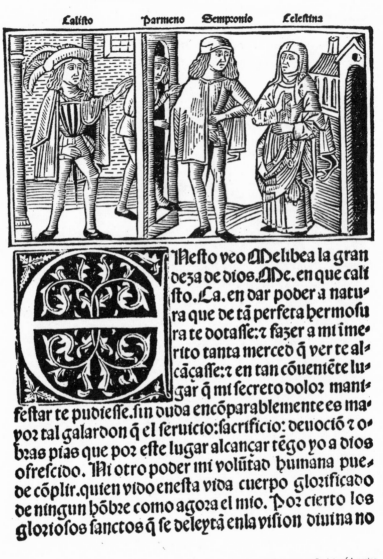

Calisto     Parmeno     Sempronio     Celestina

En esto veo Melibea la gran
deza de dios.Me. en que calí
sto.La. en dar poder a natu
ra que de tã perfeta hermosu
ra te dotasse:z fazer a mi ime
rito tanta merced q ver te al
cãçasse:z en tan cõueniẽte lu
gar q mi secreto dolor mani
festar te pudiesse.sin duda encõparablemente es ma
por tal galardon q el seruicio:sacrificio: deuociõ z o
bras pias que por este lugar alcançar tẽgo yo a dios
ofrescido. Mi otro poder mi volũtad humana pue
de cõplir.quien vido enesta vida cuerpo glorificado
de ningun hõbre como agora el mio. Por cierto los
gloriosos sanctos q se deleytã enla vision diuina no

Page of Comedia de Calisto y Melibea (Burgos, 1499)

# Fernando de Rojas

By Peter N. Dunn

*University of Rochester*

TWAYNE PUBLISHERS

A DIVISION OF G. K. HALL & CO., BOSTON

**Library of Congress Cataloging in Publication Data**

Dunn, Peter N.
    Fernando de Rojas.

    (Twayne's world authors series; TWAS 368: Spain)
    Bibliography: pp. 183–88
    Includes index.
    1. Rojas, Fernando de, d. 1541.
PQ6428.D8        868'.2'09        75–9838
ISBN 0–8057–6218–3

... a book which has won applause from every tongue.

Tomás Tamayo de Vargas, *Junta de libros*, 1624.

Who can doubt that the little book *Celestina* is one of the most witty and wise books ever written? But though the man of wit will take honey from it, the wicked will suck poison ...

Francisco Ortiz, *Apología en defensa de las comedias*, late 16th century.

... *Amadis of Gaul, Tristan of Lyonesse, Primaleon, Prison of Love*, and *Celestina* which (with many others besides) should be prohibited by law from being printed (much less sold) because their message appeals to sensuality, urging people to sin and taking their minds off virtuous living.

Bishop Antonio de Guevara, *Aviso de privados*, 1539.

# Contents

# About the Author

Peter N. Dunn has been Professor of Spanish Literature at the University of Rochester since 1966. Born in England, he completed his studies at the University of London and taught for sixteen years at the University of Aberdeen, Scotland. In 1964–65, he was Visiting Professor of Romance Languages at Case-Western Reserve University, Cleveland.

His previous books are *Castillo Solórzano and the Decline of the Spanish Novel* (1952) and an edition of Calderón's *El alcalde de Zalamea* (1966). He has also published many articles and book-reviews on Spanish literature, ranging from medieval poetry and prose through Cervantes, the seventeenth-century drama, and beyond. He has lectured in the United States and abroad.

Professor Dunn has held office in the Modern Language Association and is a member of the national council of the Renaissance Society of America. His distinctions include being awarded the degree of Doctor of Literature by the University of London, and being elected to the Academy of Literary Studies.

# Preface

The aims of this book are similar to those of other volumes in this series. Broadly stated, these aims are to acquaint the student and the general reader with the career and works of an outstanding author and to explain, as fully as may be necessary and practical, the relation of the writer to his historical moment, and his place in what we call the literary tradition. This volume, however, will differ somewhat from most of the others, for the reason that its subject cannot be made to fit any conventional format of "Life and Works."

Rojas was a one-book author whose life is largely hidden from us. The writer of a book on him is therefore precluded from discovering that he has an unexpected gift for biography. Moreover, he cannot devote a chapter to acquainting the reader with his subject's divers works; another to tracing intellectual and artistic development, changes of direction and style; a third to asking himself what qualities (if any) compose a unity in the variety of works which he has just reviewed. Instead, he faces the limitation and the challenge of writing a whole book about a single work of literature, and little else. Not that he is likely to be ungrateful: what writer of a guide to Shakespeare would not rather devote his whole book to *Hamlet*? But he is placed in an extended and intense relationship with this one work, and the danger in it is that he may forget whom he is talking to. The reader, for his part, may be unprepared for the detailed and sustained discussion of a single (and not very long) work. The challenge, then, is to guide the reader at some length without intimidating him with professional minutiae or paralyzing him with pedantry, to keep his own feet off the grass while pointing to those places where, beyond the barrier of language and style, the specialists have explored and discovered treasure.

The difficulties of writing about Rojas and *La Celestina* are not confined to the question of how to sustain the relation with a nonspecialist reader, or avoid the temptation to ride a hobby-horse through this generous expanse of chapters. *La Celestina* itself was enlarged and rewritten, and there is doubt as to what parts Rojas actually wrote. The history of its publication is full of obscurities. There are preliminaries which may or may not have been written by Rojas, and which could affect our understanding of his intention. Its form (novel? play? hybrid? or something unique?) has been a matter of controversy. So has its meaning. If the circumstantial questions, the how and the when of the book's composition and publication, must not divert attention from the work that it finally became, it is also true that these questions may not be ignored. They are the conditions of its existence and of its form. And, since there seems to be no way that they can be dispelled, they remind us of the fragility of our judgments.

In first setting out to write this book, I intended to present as faithfully as possible a summary of the various arguments and opinions on some matters of passionate controversy, and to refrain from personal intervention. Regrettably perhaps, it has not been possible to sustain this intention throughout. In chapter 4, and subsequently, it became clear that the only reading of *La Celestina* that I was qualified to elaborate was my own, and I sincerely hope that in diverging from the views of others, I have not represented them unfairly. Needless to say, my interpretation is still largely derived from other scholars, whose beneficiary I am. The reputation of every masterpiece (and *La Celestina* is a masterpiece) has its history, which is an object lesson in the fallibility of scholars—prisoners of their own times, tastes, and prejudices—each of whom hopes to be the exception who will rise above his limitations. Such a history enjoins one to modesty. The reader will not find here the final truth about *La Celestina*, and I doubt that such a thing exists. This book is meant to be a guide, not an oracle, and the greatest praise that it could receive would be the epithet "useful."

A few words on the book's arrangement. Following the chapters on Rojas, his times, and the book's own unusual story, is a series of act-by-act summaries of *La Celestina*, each summary being followed by a much longer commentary (chapter 4). These summaries follow the order of the play itself and are guided by its flow and tempo. The topics that they point to are then taken up and examined separately in a more systematic way in the following three chapters, titled "Genre and Antecedents," "Characters," and "Structures." In each of these chapters it is the distance and the angle from which the material is viewed, rather than the material itself, which is varied. For this reason, it is not essential that these chapters be read in the order of their appearance. In addition, and throughout these final chapters, I have attempted to make explicit the general literary theory within which my analysis operates, for I believe that the reader is entitled to know on what grounds one form of approach or one mode of inquiry is preferred to another, and why some matters are considered important, others not.

It is a standard requirement of this series that quotations be given in English. Several adequate modern translations of *La Celestina* exist (they are referred to in the Bibliography) and I have benefited greatly from them. However, I have chosen to offer my own translations when quoting, not because I believe them to be superior, but because (in addition to questions of copyright which arise in extensive citations) a pedantic verbal accuracy may, regrettably, be more useful than verve and elegance, for the purposes of discussion and analysis.

It remains only to observe that all references to the text are to the Spanish edition of Julio Cejador y Frauca in the series "Clásicos castellanos" (Madrid), in two volumes. Almost every quotation, whether in English or Spanish, is accompanied by the number of the volume (Roman numeral) and page of this edition, where its source is to be found. Thus the reader who wishes to go from the translated excerpt to the original can do so without difficulty.

My debts to other writers will be apparent in the text and the notes. Here I wish to record my personal thanks to my wife for her patience and for her critical eye, to Dr. Gerald Bond for his friendly suggestions, to Mrs. Janice Hyde who turned my longhand into legible script (and said she enjoyed it), and to Mr. T. E. May for conversations long ago.

PETER N. DUNN

*University of Rochester*

# Chronology

1475 or 1476 Possible date of birth of Fernando de Rojas.

1493 or 1494 Conjectured date of entry into University of Salamanca.

1498 or 1499 Likely dates for completion of Bachelor's degree, in Laws.

1498–1499 Probable period of composition of first version of *La Celestina* (*Comedia*).

1499 Earliest dated edition of *La Celestina*.

1500–1503 Extended version of *La Celestina* (*Tragicomedia*) written about this time.

1502 or 1503 Rojas left University of Salamanca without completing degree of Licentiate.

1502–1504 Likely date of lost first edition of *Tragicomedia*.

1503–1507 Resident in his native town, La Puebla de Montalbán.

1507 (perhaps earlier) Moved to Talavera de la Reina, where he spent the rest of his life as a lawyer.

??–?? Lord Mayor of Talavera.

1541 April. Died.

CHAPTER 1

# Life and Times of Fernando de Rojas

MUCH more is known about the times of Fernando de Rojas than about his life. The facts relating to him are meager, and almost nothing can be placed in time with an exact date, except his death. The age in which he lived, however, was crucial for the development of Spanish history and society. This chapter, accordingly, will take account of some of the events which occurred during Rojas' lifetime and in the periods which preceded and followed it. My purpose, however, is not simply to place him in the historical record of events by reference to familiar dates and great names, but rather to set him in his world, to locate the trends and the pressures of that world, so far as they can be ascertained and briefly told. Not historical background, but historical envelope.[1]

## I  A Career in the Law

The author, in some preliminary verses which preface *La Celestina* in all the editions from 1500 on, reveals his name, his profession, and his place of birth, by means of an acrostic: "The Bachelor [i.e., of Laws] Fernando de Rojas finished the Comedy of Calisto and Melibea and was born in La Puebla de Montalbán" (some fourteen miles to the west of Toledo). There is no document attesting to the year of his birth, no subsequent legal declaration of his age, from which the birth date might be inferred. It is also not beyond question that he was born at La Puebla, as we shall see. The little that we can base calculation upon is (1) that he held the degree of Bachelor by the year 1500 and (2) that *La Celestina* was composed after 1496. The course of study for the baccalaureate in law normally required six years, so that it is reasonable to suppose that he began his studies at Salamanca in 1493 or 1494. Stu-

13

dents usually entered university between the ages of fourteen
and sixteen years, which suggests a possible birth date of 1477
or 1478. Allowing for one's natural reluctance to attribute *La
Celestina* to an author of a mere twenty years, we might move
the date back a year or so to, say 1475 or 1476. Thus, he could
have completed his bachelor's degree around 1498–99 and have
written *La Celestina* shortly thereafter (the first edition is dated
1499). There is never any mention of his completing the degree
of Licentiate, which normally occupied a further four years, so
we must suppose that he left Salamanca perhaps in 1502–1503.
A deposition made in 1584 by a witness for Rojas' grandson,
states that Fernando de Rojas spent "some time" (*cierto
tiempo*) as a resident in La Puebla de Montalbán before moving
to Talavera, a larger town, some twenty-five miles further west,[2]
not later than 1507. This last date emerges from Rojas's own testimony for a resident of Talavera in 1517, saying that he had
known him for ten years.[3] About this time, he married Leonor
Alvarez, daughter of Alvaro de Montalbán.[4] Presumably he
was now assured a livelihood as a lawyer in what was a prosperous town. From now on, it seems safe to presume, Rojas was
a successful and increasingly influential and respected member
of the community in Talavera, though he maintained his ties of
property and family in La Puebla de Montalbán.[5] The only
record we have of his professional existence, apart from his
brief testimony in 1517, is his nomination in 1525 as attorney
by his aged father-in-law Alvaro de Montalbán, who was being
interrogated by the Inquisition. In his petition to be represented
by Rojas, the old man identifies him as his "son-in-law, resident
of Talavera, and a *converso*" (that is, a converted Jew, or
Christian of Jewish ancestry; the force of this word will become
apparent shortly). The petition was rejected.[6] A seventeenth-
century historian of Talavera states that Fernando de Rojas,
"author of Celestina," settled in the town, where he was "a
learned attorney and even became lord mayor for a number of
years."[7] He died early in April, 1541. His testament was drawn
up and signed by him on April 3 in the presence of his family,
being "sick of body but sound of memory and in full possession
of my mind and understanding."[8] The complete inventory of
possessions, from the house and the vineyard to the iron hooks

for hanging baskets, was drawn up on April 8 under the direction of Rojas' widow.[9] He must, therefore, have died very soon after April 3. He was buried in the Convent of the Mother of God (*monasterio de la Madre de Dios*) which was then a relatively recent and very modest foundation, and was wrapped in a habit of St. Francis.[10]

## II  *Personality*

Such is the modest biography of the author of one of the great works of Spanish literature. A life contained, for the most part, in the twenty-five miles or so of the valley of the Tagus, from La Puebla de Montalbán to Talavera, except for the years of study in Salamanca. The move from the small, semifeudal Puebla, dominated by the medieval castle of Montalbán and the overlordship of the Téllez Girón family, to the larger, more commercially prosperous Talavera is significant. But the significance is less in the mobility, geographic and social, of Fernando de Rojas than in the essential modesty of these changes. In times when preferment for men of humble birth could be sudden and dizzy (as part of royal policy to create an enlightened and dedicated class of functionaries free of ties with noble families), Rojas' career was scarcely meteoric. Rather, it suggests a man who was careful not to overreach himself. He had written a brilliant work in dialogue called the *Comedia de Calisto y Melibea* and, encouraged by its success among his companions, he had enlarged it into the *Tragicomedia*. From then on, he is not known to have written anything more. The *Tragicomedia* is different enough in scale and the modifications are sufficiently extensive for it to be called Rojas' second work. Yet the second is carefully built upon the first, so that one notices a frugality in his keeping everything of the original. Nothing is discarded.

His thriftiness is equally apparent in the inventory of his household in which we observe "a quantity of old wood, of about a dozen planks and beams"[11] waiting, presumably, for a new use to which they too can be put. We notice, too, the absence of any outstandingly valuable items such as jewelry or lavish clothing. The furniture is solid and

serviceable rather than elegant. He had his own set of carpen-
try tools, and the reader is impressed by the frequency with
which items are described as "old," "worn," "used," "frayed."
Finally, as noted by Careaga, Rojas apparently chose for his
burial place a poor convent rather than one of the churches
or religious houses selected by those who wished to depart this
life in a ritual display of pomp and grandeur, and leave behind
impressive monuments. No convincing answer can ever be given
to the question *why* Rojas wrote only a single book. Indeed, the
question is ultimately meaningless. But I do not think it is fanciful to see in his adoption of a preexisting act I, and in the
careful reelaboration of his own work, a personality which includes imaginative insight and a deep knowledge of his resources and of how far they will extend without strain, a personality revealed also in his leaving his native town—but not
going too far—and pursuing a professional ambition—but not
too high. Unlike Calisto in *La Celestina,* when he moves his foot
to the next rung he will be sure that the other foot remains
firmly in its place.

### III  *Salamanca*

The oldest university in Spain at that time, Salamanca was
also the largest and the most prestigious, both inside and outside
of Spain, with a wider range of studies than any other. The
life of Rojas coincided with the great period of expansion of
learning, in Spain and elsewhere. Within the span of a few
years the University of Valencia was reorganized, backed by a
new papal charter (1500), and that of Alcalá (1508), founded
on the personal initiative of the Cardenal-Inquisitor Ximénez de
Cisneros, achieved instant renown with the planning of the
great Complutensian Polyglot Bible. Salamanca and the other
universities recruited scholars from France and Italy as part of
a deliberate policy to elevate the competence and the intellectual level of men in the government of both church and
state.

Of Rojas's own presence at the University of Salamanca we
have only the barest indication, in his prefatory verses where he
says "I first saw this work in Salamanca" and in the *Letter*

which refers to his "principal study" of laws. We have no way of telling whether he was or was not impressed by professors bringing new learning from Italy (though the best years were yet to come), or what books in those days of the new printing press caused greatest intellectual excitement among the students, though it is certain that he was greatly stimulated by the Basel (1496) edition of Petrarch's *De Remediis utriusque Fortunae* (Remedies for both Good and Bad Fortune). Among his contemporaries who achieved eminence were the physician Francisco de Villalobos, the playwright and musician Lucas Fernández, and Hernán Cortés. Juan de Cervantes, grandfather of the novelist, was also a fellow student of Rojas'.

Apart from the physical hardships and spartan living which have characterized the average student everywhere until recently, and which may still be encountered in European universities, Rojas would have experienced the special rituals, the traditional routines, and the self-rewarding activities of which university life is compounded. Like most medieval universities, Salamanca was urban, and the word "campus" would be inappropriate: the pattern was the monastic cloister and the spatial nucleus the paved courtyard. This visual likeness to the conventual model also expresses the separateness of the students from the life and the laws of the city, though their boisterous gaiety often had little enough of the monastic about it. Rojas himself, referring to a section of his readers as *la alegre juventud y mancebía* ("the joyful company of the young") most likely had his student contemporaries in mind. On reading his words on the universality of strife (*Prólogo*) we should also bear in mind that while the life of a student was separate from the commerce and the concerns of the city, it was not necessarily more tranquil. Riots between "town" and "gown" have been a regular part of college life until recently, and in those parts of the world where higher education is not the natural prerogative of anyone who holds a high school diploma, the word "student" carries mingled overtones of envy, respect, and hostility. The students themselves, competing in intellectual games, in personal rivalries, in clashes of wits, in daring stunts in defiance of authority, were organized in such a way as to intensify animosities, that is, by place of origin.[12] The students elected their rector and most of their professors, and while the latter were often engaged in bitter and prolonged debates, their student supporters fought armed battles for them in the streets. In elections, each student had as many votes as his number of years of study. Thus wit, ingenuity, seniority, daring, intellectual eminence all tended to establish new patterns of relationship within a university and to submerge those social forms of alienation by which they would be separated in their native towns and villages.

Since Rojas, as we have seen, left no record of personal experiences as a student, these observations have had to be generic as well as excessively brief and schematic.[13] However, it is important to have some sense of what student life was like then (so different in many ways from that of the United States in the second half of the twentieth century), because the one work Rojas wrote was completed while he was a student. That is to say, while he was a member of a peculiar self-governing corporation which imposed on its members relationships which were distinct from those of the outside world. Like a soldier, a student had new allegiances and values which could suddenly cause the "other" world to appear abstract, arbitrary, disordered. From the temporary, and no less arbitrary perspective of the university, the "real" world was unreal. It was not the dreamlike unreality sensed by a contemporary student isolated on his campus who listens to the world on his radio, but a contrast set up in thousands of little contacts and conflicts on the city streets, in the taverns, and worked out by the students' dress codes, curfews, exemptions from city ordinances, the ambivalent attitudes of shopkeepers to transient students' requests for credit, and so on, *ad infinitum*. *La Celestina* has formal precedents in Latin comedies, as we shall see, but there are nuances which such precedents cannot explain. Such features as the dialogue's peculiar intensity, Rojas' presentation of the characters as occupying a space which is defined by their preoccupations rather than by their physical surroundings, and his readiness to dislocate characters from traditional roles—must surely have been enhanced by the sharpening of perception which accompanies the unfamiliar angle of vision on a familiar world.

Salamanca in the 1490s was also, as Gilman has pointed out, a point of transition in the movement away from a highly developed oral culture in which professors lectured, explained, and dictated; while students repeated, responded, amplified, and defended. This intellectual culture, like the folk culture which lay beneath it, was acquired and incorporated by repetition. The great novelty, of course, was printing,[14] and it is easy to overlook the fact that *Celestina* is one of the earliest examples of original imaginative literature in Spain to appear in print. Seen in this context, its mastery of oral expression and, in particular, the completeness with which Rojas could penetrate the oral style given him in act I, together with the citations from Petrarch and other authorities (like one ballad absorbing lines from another) are historically comprehensible if no less amazing.[15]

## IV  A *Changing World*

The world, of course, is always changing; and so, by implication, is man's sense of his place in it. The last years of the fifteenth century and the beginning of the sixteenth, however, present so great a number of changes and so many significant events which point to deep shifts in the structure of the intelligible world that some mention, however brief, needs to be made here. Needless to say, the change of century had nothing to do with it: there is no evidence that people expected events to proceed to cataclysmic climax in the year 1500, as they had done for the year 1000. One might easily compile a simple list of events, artists, books, etc., contemporary with our author (many of which would have been completely unknown to him at the time and, perhaps, always). This might orient the reader in relation to some familiar dates and persons, but it would probably tell him little of what this meant to the bright youth who had gone from his small country town to the big university. What follows in this section is a kind of historical shorthand for large and deep currents of change.

*Expanding horizons.* By 1500 the hitherto known boundaries of the world had been crossed, and all was open and awaiting discovery. The Portuguese Diogo Cão reached the Congo in 1482, and as for Columbus' voyages, it was more challenging to the mind to realize that the lands he discovered were not the East Indies than it would have been had he really landed in

China. And it was more disturbing to Christian orthodoxy to discover lands unconnected with any other, where the inhabitants were as well proportioned as the Spaniards, and not "men whose heads / Grew beneath their shoulders." Monsters could be fitted into traditional legends, but it was far more difficult to account for men made in the image of God who nevertheless could not have descended from Ham, Shem, or Japhet.

*Political aggrandizement.* In the same year that Columbus discovered Hispaniola and Cuba, the armies of Ferdinand and Isabella finally stormed and took the city of Granada, the last great center remaining to the Moors, and the end of their five-centuries-old occupation of Spanish soil. Ferdinand's Crown of Aragon, meanwhile, had acquired extensive territories in Italy, from Naples south to Sicily. By shrewd marriages, he would soon be followed on the throne of a united Spain by a Hapsburg, Charles, King of Spain, of the Low Countries, Emperor of Germany, Holy Roman Emperor.... To the east in Europe, to the west across the Atlantic, the energies of Spain would be released in conquest and in political dominance. And to the south, a holy war of revenge against the Arabs in Africa, long dreamed of by preachers and writers, was initiated with papal blessing on the new crusade in 1494. Cardinal Cisneros personally led the Spanish army against Oran.

*Social authoritarianism.* Ferdinand and Isabella gradually overcame the forces of powerful nobles and, in doing so, increased the central authority of the Crown, working through an increasing class of professional lawyers and administrators. Royal authority drew increasing support direct from popular sentiment which was generally far more conservative, anti-Jewish, anti-intellectual, and anticommercial than the aristocracy were. The Holy Office of the Inquisition (established in 1474 in Castile) quickly became as much an instrument of social control as of the maintenance of doctrinal purity (an institution with which Rojas' family was, unfortunately, closely acquainted—see next section, below). In 1492, the year of the conquest of Granada, the Jews were expelled from Spain, and ten years later the Moors were also, unless they accepted conversion to Christianity. From then on, the country was nominally "pure" in faith.

*Fragmented Christendom.* The Middle Ages were not the

period of absolute religious uniformity that they are sometimes believed to have been, and from the middle of the fourteenth century deviant religious movements, often with a strong social egalitarian zeal, became more fequent and more powerful. Hus, Wyclif, the Lollards, and many lesser-known individuals and groups created intense strains in Catholic Europe. Other forms of reaction against the Roman institution took a more devotional turn, like the lay evangelism of the Brethren of the Common Life, among whom Erasmus was educated, or the revival of pagan mysteries among Florentine intellectuals. Even the institional Church of Rome had been sadly shaken by the Great Schism (1378–1417) and the scandal of the three popes; and the conciliar movement for reform during the fifteenth century had caused popes to seek in Italian politics, ostentatious luxury, and personal ruthlessness, the authority which seemed so hard to sustain in the spiritual domain.[16] Rojas was a contemporary of many reformers and sympathizers with new spiritual movements: Erasmus (1465–1536), Luther (1483–1546), Alonso de Valdés (1490?–1532) and his brother Juan (1500?–1541) among others.

*Displacement of values and new models of representation.* Social changes are accompanied by changes in the way people evaluate themselves, their acts, and their property. Increasing wealth, growth of towns, and a middle class owing its livelihood to the exchange of goods and money rather than ownership of land are features of the fifteenth century. Material things, lands, servants, come to be valued in important circles as means of personal display rather than as symbols of a man's service, his honor, or his dependence upon God and king.[17] In *La Celestina* we can observe a tension between these two kinds of value—the commercial and the symbolic. Also, the increased value given to man in relation to a God-given world, of which Pico della Mirandola's *De hominis dignitate* (Oration on the Dignity of Man, 1486?)[18] is often taken to be a significant example, marks a shift of focus in the arts. The Dutch painters like Jan van Eyck showed men in their real daily surroundings, kitchens, living rooms, workshops, tilled fields, and windmills to be fit subjects for art. Linear perspective, which came to dominate pictorial composition during the late fifteenth century, emphasizes and dignifies the real world by setting objects in their own space, rather than disposing them on a flat surface according to their symbolic value. Again, we may observe that *La Celestina* creates an autonomous world of talk related to the immediate concerns of the speakers; yet at the same time it retains important elements of traditional symbolism.

In this summary we have made no mention of scientific discovery or technical advances, because very little had taken place. The great new technique was printing, as we have noted already, and by its means a book written in Paris or Basel or Naples could be disseminated across Europe in a matter of months. But the great scientific advances, like the great territorial discoveries on the other side of the world, came later on in Rojas' life, not during the time of his intellectual formation. In fact, we might say that he was a student during a period of intellectual conservatism. Copernicus (1473–1543) was an almost exact contemporary of Rojas, but there could be no "Copernican revolution" until the ancient systems of Ptolemy and Aristotle had been thoroughly studied by men who knew their Greek and so could clear away traditional misinterpretations. Then, when that was done, what Ptolemy and Aristotle really said could be tested by observation. In the same way, medicine and anatomy waited upon the textual experts ("humanists" in the narrow sense) to provide Galen's treatises on anatomy, instead of medieval Latin digests, before Vesalius, Fracastoro, Agricola, and the rest in that great century could seek alternative theoretical structures for their observations.[19]

In attempting thus briefly to indicate the points of growth and change in Rojas' world we must be careful not to read the later sixteenth century back into the 1490s. Spain was not yet a great empire, and the trans-Atlantic world was as yet only glimpsed. But precisely because the growing points could not yet reveal the nature of the flower, the possible enlargement of a world of action and thought pressing against a world of increasingly far-reaching institutions and administrative powers could generate a sense of uncertain excitement. There is a pattern of frustration in *La Celestina* as well as a much smaller element of rejuvenation: the common stereotype of a "Renaissance optimism" which supposedly accompanied scientific and artistic achievement (and which is a self-serving concept, a way of congratulating ourselves and putting technical pursuits above all humane values) overlooks the fact that the common experiences of men and women in their struggles to live have not changed. Moreover, the great innovations of Rojas' formative years were not in the investigation or control of the natural world, but in the control of men and society—in administration, diplomacy, and warfare. Ferdinand, the most notorious monarch of his time, had the reputation of out-lying even Louis XI of France and deceiving his own ambassadors at the same time. The most notorious writer, Machiavelli, merely observed the secularization of the state and reasoned accordingly. His behavioristic view of politics was more likely to derive from, and conduce to, a social pessimism than its opposite, since it removed from public affairs the umbrella of a divinely ordered providence. *La Celestina* is not an optimistic work.

## V  *Fathers and Sons*

In Rojas' own words, in the acrostic formed by the introductory verses of *La Celestina*, he was born in La Puebla de Montalbán. Since there are no baptismal records, his ancestry has to be traced from other documents, notably the sworn testimony of his descendants and witnesses on various occasions. Two of these were in connection with petitions by Rojas' grandson, also named Fernando, and a lawyer, for a *probanza de hidalguía* ("certificate of gentlemanly status") in 1567[20] and 1584.[21] For this purpose a number of local residents, old people with long memories, were called upon to give testimony that they knew the family, the applicant's father and grandfather (the author) and great grandfather. They all obligingly confirmed that the Rojas family had owned land, had been recognized as hidalgos, and had enjoyed exemption from taxes. Most witnesses could not recall the author's father, but a few were more positive: one recalled a time when the name of Garci González de Rojas was familiar to all the old inhabitants. This Garci González was said to have come to settle in La Puebla de Montalbán from the village of Tineo in Asturias, the mountainous northern province. His mother was Catalina de Rojas, and nothing is known about her. The same information, naturally enough, is given in the *Libro de memorias* compiled by the grandson Fernando. However, as stated earlier, Alvaro de Montalbán requested in 1525 that he be legally represented by his son-in-law "the Bachelor Fernando de Rojas who wrote *Celestina,* and who is a converso." When Manuel Serrano y Sanz in 1902 published the trial documents he was of the opinion, lacking other evidence, that Rojas would most likely have been born of a mixed marriage, inheriting the Jewish blood from his father since status is determined by the paternal line.[22] Now, we find the grandson compiling documents showing that the family can be traced back to Asturias. Such a claim, if it were true, would be accepted as sufficient evidence of *limpieza de sangre* ("cleanness of blood"), which meant Christian ancestry with no intermingling of Jewish or Moorish blood. How are these opposing statements to be reconciled?

Here we must rely heavily on the documents uncovered by Professor Gilman and put together in his *The Spain of Fernando de Rojas.* In 1606 one Hernán Suárez Franco, a distant cousin of the Rojas, pressed legal proceedings for an *ejecutoria* (title of hidalgo). After a lengthy investigation, the petition was rejected in the most crushing terms: the petitioner and his family had to pay the costs of the inquiry, the search for documents, etc., and were condemned to "perpetual silence," that is, they were never to reopen their claim. One of the documents, which were usual in such a case, was a family tree drawn up by the claimants and then subjected to critical scrutiny by the investigating judge. In this case the family tree was broad enough to embrace the Rojas as well as the Francos, and it included Rojas' presumed father Garci Gonzalez de Rojas. On the copy seen by Gilman, the investigating judge (*fiscal*) has noted against the name of Rojas: "The Bachelor Rojas who composed Celestina. The *fiscal* contends that he was a son of Hernando de Rojas condemned as a *judaizante* in the year '88. . . ."[23]

*Judaizante* is a very broad term. It could mean one who, though baptized a Christian, has secretly practiced the Jewish religion, or it could mean one who in some respect of his dietary habits or his clothing has followed traditions of his Jewish ancestors, without prejudice to his Christian beliefs.

In the years before 1492 (when Jews were expelled from Spain) whole towns and villages might be predominantly populated by a mixture of Jews and conversos, and the latter would often still fraternize with the former or buy from the same butcher. There might have been no priest capable of preparing converts adequately and no butcher or tailor other than Jewish ones. The arrival of the Inquisition could turn such misfortunes or natural relationships into crimes. The judge's note continues with a reference to the grandson Fernando de Rojas, "for whom they contrived an Asturian great-grandfather." The judge, it appears, had consulted the records of the Inquisition and discovered that Rojas' father had been condemned in 1488. He was also acquainted with the evidence collected about his family history in 1567 and 1584 by the grandson, now dead. Garci González would then be an honorable ancestor fraudulently replacing the dishonorable one in the family history. Such was the anxiety about lineage by the end of the sixteenth century that ancestor-substitution was by no means unusual. If this information were in the records of the Inquisition, it is easy to understand why the grandson Fernando de Rojas, a lawyer of the Court of Chancery in Valladolid, "a kind of supreme court of social privilege and exemption,"[24] did not proceed with his own suit for a title of hidalgo beyond the preliminary gathering of testimony. We do not know what the Licenciate Rojas really knew about his family history. The records of the Inquisition were highly secret, but in his position he may have been given just enough of a hint to realize that a falsification of family lineage was not going to stand up to scrutiny and so withdrew the petition. On the other hand, the judge may have been mistaken (there were a great many Rojas in the jurisdiction of Toledo) or malicious. In any case, Rojas would have been unable to challenge such damaging inferences because of the secrecy with which the Inquisition always protected its evidence.[25] As Gilman has shown, the author's unfortunate father-in-law who was condemned to perpetual house arrest for some indiscreet words, later disappeared from the family tree, to be replaced by a Dr. Juan Alvárez (who, in reality, belongs to a later generation).[26]

## VI   *Jews and Conversos*

We now need to explain why it should be so desirable to conceal an ancestor. What was the standing of the conversos and what was the relation between the Inquisition and public opinion?[27] Large numbers of Jews had accepted conversion to Christianity during the fifteenth century after the terrible anti-Jewish massacres of 1391, though there had been earlier mass conversions in 1369. In spite of popular jealousy and hatred, the Jewish community had enjoyed a high degree of prestige, providing trusted treasurers and administrators to the Crown of Castile and also to many aristocratic families. They married into the nobility, and their wealth and influence often gave them powerful positions on large city councils. Of those who converted to Christianity, some entered the church, or saw their sons do so, and rise to positions of eminence. Thus, the families of conversos may have enjoyed greater power and influence and wealth than they had before conversion. Such a state of things was far from stable, for it aroused the hostility of both the Jews who refused to abandon Judaism, and the Old Christians who felt that they were being cheated of privileges by newcomers who were barely disguised Jews. Conversos achieved great prominence at the courts of kings John II and Henry IV of Castile; Pablo de Santa María passed from being rabbi of Burgos to bishop of the same city. The fifteenth century, however, brought mounting violence; revolts of conversos in Toledo, against discriminatory taxation and other forms of oppression, in 1449 and 1467 (reprisals destroyed 1,600 of their homes in the latter year); battles in Vallodolid, in 1470, and throughout Andalusia in the 1470s. A papal bull *Humanis generis* (September, 1449) prohibited all insults and forms of discrimination against conversos but was clearly ineffective. The principal consequences of these violent conditions which involved both Jews and conversos were the following.

    1. Royal exploitation of Jews; Isabella accepted subsidies from the Jewish community in exchange for protection.

    2. In spite of these promises, Isabella ordered the expulsion of Jews who did not accept Christianity, on March 30, 1492.

    3. Old Christians throughout the sixteenth century worked for

the exclusion of conversos from public offices, religious orders, fraternities, and ranks of nobility, often against powerful resistance from influential and reasonable men. It is important to realize that not only the new converts were the object of this effort at discrimination but *descendants of converts in perpetuity.* The great grandson of a convert was still a converso in the language of the time.

4. Thus, although a Jew may have turned Christian in 1391 or 1474, his descendants would still be reputed as conversos, and therefore subject to civil disabilities, which increased in the course of the sixteenth century.

5. The Holy Office of Inquisition, for which papal permission was obtained in 1478, was established in Castile. Its purpose was not to harass Jews and Moors but to deal with the "new Christians" who originated in both religions and who might be suspected of secretly lapsing into their former beliefs or practices. (Later, it directed its energies to persons suspected of Protestant heresies, and witchcraft.)

We are not concerned here with the economic consequences of the expulsion of the Jews but with mapping out the oppressive social relations which were created, and the means by which the conversos might seek to escape them. Spain was not the only nation to exploit and to persecute Jews; what was peculiar to Spain (and Portugal, though perhaps to a lesser extent) was the social branding of persons of Jewish descent, generation after generation, though they might be convinced and practicing Christians. Briefly and with crude oversimplification, we may say that the expansion of Castile in the Middle Ages, achieved by overrunning the territories held by the Moors and by turning the Arab concept of the religious war into a crusade, created an adversary mentality. Both territorial progress, and the sense of collective moral superiority which a long period of war requires, were measured by reference to the Moorish enemy. When this traditional enemy no longer existed as a threat within the geographical boundaries of Spain, the same pattern of directed energies carried Cisneros with an army into Africa and turned the civilian population against the "aliens" within. Just as certain totalitarian societies in the twentieth century have needed internal "fascist" or "communist" enemies (not to mention Jews), so the old Christians of Castile[28] needed the presence of this separate caste.[29] The old Christians' mentality was formed predominantly in the countryside among small farmers, sheepherders, and village gentry, and also among some artisans of the towns who were in direct competition with converso craftsmen. The merchants and traders and bankers were predominantly of Jewish background or had Jewish family connections. Thus the converso problem was part racial, part economic and social. Old Christians were of the country, conversos were of the towns, with an overlap in the artisan class. During the preceding centuries of reconquest, Christians had maintained their separate identity in the face of the material superiority of Arabic culture by asserting the moral superiority of frugality and asceticism. Thus, the old Christians were (and again I acknowledge the crude generalization) historically conditioned not only to oppose and to resist the converso but also to retain him as a necessary irritant rather than to supplant him. By shaming him they could define their own superiority, impose their own kind of exclusiveness from below, and express their economic resentments.

When the Inquisition was established, with the purpose of defending the faith by preventing lapses into Judaism, it was not capable of covering the whole country immediately but was installed region by region as its bureaucracy was extended. It was set up in the jurisdiction of Toledo in 1484 and, as was usual, proclaimed an Edict of Grace. This meant that persons were free to come forward and confess offenses against the Christian faith, in the understanding that they would be pardoned, after due penance, and reconciled to the Church. This appears simple enough, but when the edict was proclaimed in a town or district it was not solely a matter of confessing if one had something to confess or staying home. The individual who confessed had also to tell whatever he knew, or suspected, against anyone else of his acquaintance. Failure to speak up (e.g., failure to accuse yourself of what someone else had accused you; failure to accuse X of what Y would later accuse X) could be construed as perjury or as conspiracy and could carry the gravest consequences. "The knowledge that one was vulnerable to accusations" observes Gilman, "created a kind of chain reaction in which the hapless candidates for 'reconciliation' were induced to tell all they knew or suspected about their relatives" (*The Spain,* p. 77). One could prove good faith to the Inquisition only by breaking faith with oneself. And "reconciliation" was not the reconciling ritual that the first penitents might have expected, because nothing was forgotten or forgiven; they were made to walk barefoot to church, Sunday after Sunday, in distinctive dress, and a record of their shame was on view for future generations, while they themselves were exposed to the jeering humiliation of their old Christian neighbors. The gossip-laden bitterness and envy of small-town life were screwed up to a pitch that is difficult to imagine. There were critics—mostly cautious and well placed—such as the historian Mariana, who, in the next century, observed that the Inquisition was unprecedented in condeming men to death for small deviations from the norm, and who was shocked that the sins of the fathers should be endlessly visited on the children. Since the sources of accusations were not revealed to the accused, there easily developed a sort of symbiosis of the Inquisition and the legion of gossips, malcontents and relentless keyhole spies. X lowers his head in church, and his enemies report that he "bows like a Jew" (*ibid.,* p. 95).

## VII   *The Rojas and Reputation*

Rojas' father-in-law was accused in 1525; the accusation against him was that he was overheard to have said that "one had better make the most of his life, since we know nothing about the next."[30] The old man was past seventy, and his responses to questions about his childhood in La Puebla in the 1460s show how the world had changed. As a child he ran about the synagogue with the Jewish children and wore the same dress they did. Under relentless questioning he could only say that he did not remember why, with what intention, he did these things, so natural at that time and now so fraught with sinister consequences. The family humiliations are revealed in the transcript of his testimony: the bodies of both his parents were burnt by the Inquisition after their deaths.[31]

Another, lurid, sidelight is thrown by an earlier humiliation of the Rojas family in 1616, when a certain Juan Francisco Palavesín y Rojas was candidate for a canonry in the Cathedral of Toledo. That cathedral chapter was the most jealously guarded place of privilege, and candidates were most rigorously investigated for any taint in their ancestry. In the course of investigation, an enemy of the candidate "accused" him of blood relationship with the Rojas of La Puebla de Montalbán and Talavera (which was proved false) and declared that those Rojas as well as those who remained in Toledo *no era gente limpia* ("were unclean"). It is notable that witnesses favorable to the candidate express "nausea," "disgust," and vehement indignation at the suggestion that he was related to the Francos or those Rojas. Notes Gilman: "In spite of more than a hundred years of scrupulously Christian behavior, two depositions of *hidalguía,* and three changes of residence, the family reputation was still hopelessly clouded."[32]

Putting all this together, it is easy to understand why the descendants of the author would stop short in the process of trying to acquire documentary validation of a claim to *hidalguía,* and rest content with a file of friendly witnesses. It is also readily appreciated that in a family tree Rojas' descendants would substitute a "safe" ancestor from Asturias (since many northern towns had expelled all Jews and conversos in the fifteenth century, and those parts had the reputation of good "clean" Christian stock). Poor old Alvaro de Montalbán, Rojas' father-in-law, was eliminated in this way. Another sentence from Gilman summarizes the situation of the conversos: "Suspicious of each other, suspected by everyone else, the conversos lived in a world in which no human relationship could be counted on, in which a single unpremeditated sentence could bring unalterable humiliation and unbearable torture. It was a world in which one had constantly to observe oneself from an alien point of view, that of the watchers from without" (*The Spain,* p. 104). The successful converso was the one who covered his past, or who got accepted without any shameful incidents before the ranks of the "establishment" closed: like the Inquisitors Torquemada and Deza, who certainly proved their loyalty beyond any possibility of doubt. Let us reiterate: it was the socially orthodox, the old Christians and the successful conversos who were able to cross over into their ranks, who operated the system of exclusions, imposed their definition of "honor," and gave to words like *honrado* ("honorable"), *limpio* ("clean"), *opinión* ("reputation") a racial tinge, and *villano* ("peasant") became a word of approbation, because Jews did not till the soil. So the illiterate peasant was preferred above the Jewish intellectual and his descendants.[33] In this reversible world of appearances, genuine ancestors disappeared and were replaced by others fraudulently adopted. One betrayed oneself in order to prove good faith; and one continually attempted to efface oneself in order not to appear different. It is no wonder that the great figures of art and literature in this period, Spain's "Age of Gold," are so creatively preoccupied with the modes of unreality, self-deception, conformity, and the problems of sustaining a self in a given society. Perhaps it is no wonder either (though in another sense all art is wonder and escapes every determinism) that Rojas expresses his art through a dialogue, in which the speakers are so deeply aware of their own motives, and the reader so uncertain about the author's.

4. A woodcut illustration, which varies from edition to edition.

5. The illustration is accompanied by an extended title:

Here follows the Comedy of Calisto and Melibea, composed as a rebuke to those foolish lovers who are so carried away by their unbridled passions that they make their mistresses their Gods. Also as a warning against the wiles of procuresses and wicked flattering servants.

6. This is followed by the "Summary of the Whole Work" ("Argumento de toda la obra"):

Calisto was of noble descent, high intelligence, elegant bearing, exquisite upbringing and many natural gifts, and was of middle rank. He fell in love with Melibea, a young noble lady of exalted ancestry enjoying the most lofty position, sole heir to her father Pleberio, and beloved of her mother Alisa. Spurred on by his passion and aided by the wicked, cunning Celestina with two of his servants whom she lured into disloyalty through their greed for money and pleasure, Calisto overcame Melibea's chaste resistance. So the lovers and those who abetted them came to a disastrous and bitter end. To begin the story, ill fortune brings together Calisto and Melibea whom he desires.

7. Following the text, as we noted above, are the verses that state the year and place of printing and also inform the reader that the author's name can be found in the other verses, those which precede the play. At this point, then, we have three pieces of information: the final verses were written by Alonso de Proaza; the author of the whole is Fernando de Rojas, Bachelor of Law; Rojas did not write act I but found it ready-made. There are some clues which point to an edition of Salamanca, 1500, but the next surviving one is Seville, 1501. This resembles the Toledo edition of 1500 very closely, both in the text and in the preliminaries.

Some time after 1501 the sixteen acts were increased to twenty-one, and the title *Comedia* changed to *Tragicomedia*. In addition, a new prologue was inserted after the acrostic verses, which purports to explain the changes. The principal change in the text is a single long interpolation which runs from what was near the end of act XIV to part way through what now becomes act XIX. But there are also many other changes, from simple words to whole paragraphs in other parts of the play. It is no exaggeration to say that the *Tragicomedia* is a different work from the *Comedia*. This is one of the teasing aspects of the book's history, for we do not know when the additions were written. Furthermore, Rojas' avowal in the prologue that they were written to satisfy the promptings of friends does not satisfy our curiosity about his own artistic judgment in the matter. This is a question which we must judge for ourselves.

These inserted passages by which the *Comedia* was metamorphosed into the *Tragicomedia* are often called the "additions of 1502," and such a phrase seemed convenient until very recently. The earliest date to be found on the long version was indeed 1502, and there were no less than six different editions all bearing that date, and each of them survives in a single unique copy. Of these six, four were printed in Seville, one in Salamanca, and one in Toledo. It was a good year for printers of *Celestina*, on the face of it. However, the rhymed colophon— the verses at the end of the book, stating place and date of origin—was not regularly changed, as has been recently discovered. Unlike the brief words and numerals usually found on the last sheet, a rhyming colophon requires some ingenuity. It is not easy to change date and place and still keep the number of syllables required by the metrical structure of the verse. And printers, then, as now, tried to cut costs. Other criteria, then, must be found for dating these six editions bearing the year 1502. In brief, study of the physical characteristics of the books—paper, type, layout, illustrations, for example—shows that not one of these "1502" editions could have been printed in that year.[3] Of the four "Seville, 1502" printings, three probably belong to the years 1511, 1513–15, and 1518–20, whereas the last was not printed in Seville at all, but in Rome, possibly in 1516.[4] The "Toledo, 1502" probably belongs to the years 1510–14. Finally, the "Salamanca, 1502" was not printed at Salamanca but in Rome, by the Spanish printer Antonio de Salamanca, between the years 1520 and 1525.

There still remains the question, when was the first edition of the *Tragicomedia*? It is possible, of course, that there really was a 1502 *Tragicomedia* published in Seville, or elsewhere. Some scholars have tried to place it further back in time, claiming that the lost Salamanca, 1500 was the first *Tragicomedia*. This would have to rest on the unlikely supposition that a competing printer would continue to market the old *Comedia* after the new version was selling. In fact, the *Comedia* was quickly forgotten and only rediscovered in 1836, and it did not become generally known until R. Foulché-Delbosc edited it in 1902. Now that all the "1502" editions have been shown to be much later, the earliest surviving edition of the *Tragicomedia* is that of Zaragoza, 1507. This cannot have been the first, however; Zaragoza is a most unlikely city for Rojas to have chosen for a completely new version of his work. Besides, the long form had already appeared in the Italian translation by Alfonso Ordóñez (Rome, 1506). So, by a strange twist in this tangled history, the earliest existing *Tragicomedia* is not in Spanish but in Italian! Furthermore, the Spanish original which it most faithfully reflects is later than itself—Valencia, 1514![5] If the true history is ever uncovered, and an earlier *Tragicomedia* brought to light, Valencia would be a likely place of printing. Proaza moved there in 1504; Ordóñez had been personally associated with the Valencian printer Joffre (who prepared the Valencia *Celestinas* of 1514 and 1518) before going to Italy.

The only change in the text of *La Celestina* which was to take place after the publication of the *Tragicomedia* (apart from the many variants[6] which inevitably appear in old texts because of faulty copying and so on) was the interpolation of an extra act. This new act, the *auto de Traso*, became act XIX in the edition of Toledo, 1526. It is named after the new character, Traso, whom the cowardly Centurio tries to persuade to carry out his promise to avenge the death of Celestina. It is attributed to one Sanabria, from whose play it is extracted, but neither author nor play (a free stage adaptation of *Celestina?*) has been identified. Only two later editions repeat the innovation, and we shall not take it into account.

## II   *The Success of* La Celestina

Bibliophiles of the last two centuries have reported seeing copies of editions of *Celestina* not recorded elsewhere. It is impossible to know how many editions were printed in Spanish,[7] but one hundred for the sixteenth century alone is not unreasonable and may be on the low side. The fact is that *Celestina* was one of the phenomenal successes of its own or any other time; nothing like it occurred again until the growth of general literacy in the last hundred years. The small numbers of specimens which survive from a great number of editions suggest that it was literally read to pieces. There could have been no one who was capable of reading who did not read *La Celestina*. This is a success which could have been matched only by the whole tribe of the novels of chivalry in the sixteenth century. After 1630 its popularity declined, but there has never been a time since its first appearance when it was not in circulation. The Spanish Inquisition and the royal censors had little quarrel with it, and the only parts to appear on the *Index* (and then not until 1632) were a few phrases in which Calisto blasphemes in praise of the "divinity" of Melibea. This is not to say that the work was completely beyond controversy or reproach. The humanist intellectual Juan Luis Vives in his Latin *De institutione foeminae christianae* (On the Education of a Christian Woman, 1520) lumped *La Celestina* in with novels of chivalry, bawdy ballads, and all other kinds of inflammatory material that should be kept from young girls. Vives (the friend of John Colet and Thomas More) had a strong puritan streak and dismissed all secular literature as frivolous, if not dangerous.

No doubt many other persons held a similar opinion, especially since the play has a degree of erotic frankness which is unusual for its time in serious literature, and since this aspect (as frequently happens) was taken up and emphasized by a host of imitators. Cervantes, in some burlesque verses which he put at the front of *Don Quijote,* declared "*Celestina,* in my opinion a heavenly book if it didn't show so much of the sensual side...."[8] Such reservations, however, were of small importance. Most intelligent readers presumably judged that the scabrous parts contributed to or were "redeemed by" (in the jargon of our present-day defense lawyers) the moral sense of the whole. If, as we saw in the last chapter, the Inquisition was a powerful instrument for maintaining social and intellectual conformity, it did little to restrict artistic expression. Its mission was to protect the faith. As to morals, and determining what may or may not be portrayed, Spain has always been a society in which public shame and the avoidance of scandal have had a strong inhibiting effect. A result of this has been a powerful urge to self-censorship both in individuals and in the small communities that make up the larger society. In this, Spain was not much different from most other nonurban, nonindustrialized societies where personal bonds still have preeminence over the "objective" ties of legal authority and of service rendered as money. It is surprising, perhaps, to find the jurist and historian Jerónimo Zurita writing a report for the Holy Office in which he recommends that profane literature be left unmolested so long as it is well written and so long as it reveals the author's moral integrity.[9] Only as the end of its existence approached did the Inquisition in its dying gasp prohibit the *Celestina* entirely (February, 1793). By that time, the book's fortunes were at their lowest, for eighteenth-century taste valued regularity and elegance, and took a narrow view of social portraits and the permissible range of dramatic action.

### III  *Revival of Interest in* La Celestina: *Modern Editions*

In the nineteenth century *La Celestina* attracted attention once again. German literary romanticism and German scholarship were influential in Spain as in other parts of Europe, with the result that the literature of Spain's Golden Age and especially the drama and the ballad poetry (those kinds of literature, that is, which give an impression of nonliterary spontaneity and popular inspiration) began to fascinate young writers and also to deserve the attention of historical and philological scholarship. In 1822, León Amarita published the first edition recorded in more than a century. It had no particular merit other than being first, but it created awareness of the need for other, better ones. In 1841 Tomás Gorchs published in Barcelona the Zaragoza edition of 1507, which, as we have noted, has a special authority in the textual tradition of the *Tragicomedia* now that all the "1502" editions have been discredited. In 1899–1900 the edition of Valencia, 1514 was published, with variants and other bibliographical apparatus, by Menéndez Pelayo. With the reediting of Burgos 1499 and Seville 1501 by Foulché-Delbosc most of the important early editions had been made available. Since then, the Toledo, 1500 and one of the Seville, "1502" texts have been edited. The publication and study of these editions brought the problems into focus. What was the *Comedia* as Rojas wrote it? When did he expand *Comedia* into *Tragicomedia*? What is the relation between the various published versions of *Tragicomedia*? Do they, perhaps, reflect different manuscripts, and if so, what would Rojas have accepted and what would he have repudiated? We have not come very far in answering these questions. It is generally agreed that Burgos, 1499 is the earliest existing edition, but not everyone is yet convinced that there was not an earlier one, now lost.[10]

Meanwhile many popular editions have appeared since the turn of the century, and some others for the student of literature or interested general reader. One of these, by Julio Cejador y Frauca, first published in 1913, was adopted by the series "Clásicos castellanos" and has been continuously in print. Starting from Foulché-Delbosc's edition of Burgos 1499, he inserted into it the *Tragicomedia* additions which he took from Valencia, 1514. We noted earlier that the latter appears now to be one of the better *Tragicomedia* editions, though Cejador cannot have known this, and his procedure would have seemed arbitrary at the time. In fact, his composite text may well be, by lucky caprice, the closest it is possible to get to the original *Tragicomedia* at present. One thing is sure, no future editor will be able to deliver a good edition with such a lucky shot. The bibliographical studies of the last thirty years have become ever more weighty, and the theoretical relationships between editions ever more complex. Professor Herriott's 1964 study lists more than ten thousand variants in twelve early editions; yet his enormous labors are still only preliminaries to a further investigation, as his title shows.

## IV   *Imitations and Continuations*

As mentioned earlier, the enormous popularity of *La Celestina* spawned numerous imitations and continuations, as well as exercising enormous influence on later writers. Some of those sequels and imitations may be noted here. Leaving aside adaptations of the original *Celestina* for stage, renderings into verse, and other oddities, the first notable independent work is the *Comedia Thebayda* (1504),[11] a long and rambling amorous adventure in fifteen scenes, which ends happily in a marriage. Obscenity and the moral compensations of a socially approved ending are the characteristics of many of the imitations. Feliciano de Silva, a prolific writer, author of such novels of chivalry as *Amadís de Grecia* and *Florisel de Niquea*, and imitator of whatever happened to be in fashion, composed his *Segunda comedia de Celestina* in 1534. In this extravagant work the author literally resurrected the old woman Celestina, who was killed in Rojas' original, and had her return to her former activities among her old associates. Again, we may note the author's desire to have the best of both worlds—a diabolical central character and scenes of erotic provocation, with stories of noble lovers who come to a virtuous end. The explanation of how the "dead" Celestina is restored to life is withheld until the final pages and is less obvious than might have been expected. The *Tercera parte de la tragicomedia de Celestina* (Third Part of Celestina, 1536) by Gaspar Gómez, continues from Silva's *Second Part*, and, once again, combines brothel scenes, the wild language of ruffians and whores, and the noble youths whose loves come to a happy conclusion. Celestina herself finally falls to her death. It is clear that the imitators are unable to write a work of artistic worth and originality, otherwise they would not keep exploiting the person of Celestina as they do. Rather, they cultivate popular taste in two different modes—first, bawdy-house jokes and a variety of low characters, and second, the novel of sentiment which was in great vogue in the later fifteenth century. There is no need to review all of them here—*Comedia Hipólita*, *Comedia Seraphina* (1521), *Tragicomedia de Lisandro y Roselia* (1542), *Tragedia Policiana* (1547), *Comedia Florinea* (1554), *Comedia Selvagia* (1554), and others besides.[12] They are an undistinguished lot, largely parasitic on earlier works.

### V　*In the Wake of* Celestina: *A Movement towards Antiheroic and Realist Fiction*

Taken in contrast with other highly popular types, however—novels of chivalry, pastoral novels, introspective novels of sentiment—it is clear that they have an interesting place in the history of literature. Though they are not in a true sense realistic, much of their crudity does express a desire to create the illusion of realism, and to include it, without moral strings, in a larger form, even if the story which envelops it comes to an impeccably moral conclusion. In the novels of chivalry, violence is heroic and, at the same time, unbelievable; incredible cardboard heroes like Amadís, Lisuarte, Palmerín, and the rest perform incredible feats in vague, shadowy regions with fanciful names, dotted with castles and palaces, but never a peasant in sight. The sequels to *Celestina* provide one kind of backlash; in them violence is not heroic, and it is often believable. The rape of Aminta (*Thebayda*, scene 10) has no artistic necessity to justify it. It is there, in abundant detail, for its own sake. Within the patent absurdities, the high-flown rhetoric, the contrived adventures which make up the greater part of these books, a desire to entertain (and be entertained) by means of the ugly, the brutal, and the coarse is enabled to find its place and its expression. One author attempts to mimic in print the words of a boy sobbing and talking at the same time; and elsewhere, a child speaks in baby talk.[13] The urge to represent and see represented commonplace, vulgar, or repugnant persons and scenes has broken through the conventions of Spanish fiction. This intrusion of the ordinary, the trivial, the unbeautiful into a world of art formed in a mold which was predominantly Platonic will itself become a convention influencing fiction and drama.

## VI  *Lope de Vega's* Dorotea

To return to *La Celestina* and its progeny, the single work which stands out from all the others is Lope de Vega's *La Dorotea* (1632).[14] This work, characterized as neither comedy nor tragicomedy but as "prose action" (*acción en prosa*) was composed in the course of many years. Like some other authors in the tradition of *Celestina*, Lope abandoned the formal division into an indeterminate number of acts and restricted himself to the academically respectable number of five, with subdivisions into scenes. Lope was a master of theater but tried to excel in every literary form—epic poetry, novel, novella, lyric, etc., etc. *La*

*Dorotea* is a hybrid: a fiction that has no narrative, a drama which (unlike the rest of his theater) is not in verse and is unactable. Also, it is intensely autobiographical. The story is of a passionate young poet Fernando in love with the beautiful Dorotea, who is manipulated by her gold-digging mother and her friend Gerarda (a heavy-drinking demi-Celestina) into a liaison with a rich colonial. Like Calisto in the *Celestina*, Fernando tries to live a romantic, literary idea of love, but his fate is not Calisto's. His love, which he believes is so noble and prepared for sacrifice, turns cynically in search of another woman in order to be free of Dorotea. The rich rival is murdered, so Dorotea, the real victim, is left unhappy and alone. In this story it is easy to see Lope revising an experience of his youth, his notorious affair with Elena Osorio, the wife of a theater manager. Yet the real Lope eludes the reader at every turn. He is reliving his experiences in the lives of a new group of invented characters, giving the feelings and acts of his vanished past the literary substance and duration which neither the young Lope nor the fictional Fernando could achieve in their respective "lives."

CHAPTER 3

# The Problems of Authorship

## I *Who Wrote Act I?*

NOW that we have surveyed the history of the book *La Celestina*, the stages of its growth, and a few of the more obvious marks it has left on subsequent literary history, we must address ourselves to another set of problems. These concern the various parts of which the book is composed and the question of Rojas' authorship of all, or only some, of them. It will be recalled that the *Comedia* consists of sixteen acts, that Rojas claims not to have written act I, and that there are various preliminaries (including the acrostic), and some terminal verses (by Alonso de Proaza). The *Tragicomedia* has five additional acts inserted, as well as many other additions to the original sixteen, an extra prologue, and some lines in Proaza's rhymed colophon. There are two principal matters of contention: (1) did Rojas really find act I ready-made, as he said, or might he have had some reason, serious or playful, for seeming to disown it? and (2) did Rojas write the additions which make the *Tragicomedia*, or has someone done to his *Comedia* what he says he did to another man's act I?

Rojas himself must bear some of the responsibility for the confusion and controversy surrounding his work. It should seem reasonable to take Rojas' word for it, that he did not write act I, and yet his manner of telling us is not quite direct, his explanation incomplete and elusive. "A person who is absent from his native place thinks back to what it lacks or needs, in order then to be able to pay his own debt of gratitude by helping to remedy the lack. Knowing how my birthplace and you [the "friend" to whom this letter is addressed] are infected with this evil of amorous passion, I saw a defense against it in the present work. The more I read it, the more I was affected by its

43

story, its style, its moral axioms, . . . so I completed it. If the
original author chose to conceal his name from malicious tongues,
do not blame me for doing the same." (That is a partial translation and condensation of I, 3–6.) If we accept this literally,
the work could not have appeared more obligingly, apparently
from nowhere, to satisfy the need of the historical moment;
and not the collective historical moment only, but Rojas' own
frame of mind as he contemplaed his historical situation. Rojas'
argument follows a logic of design and final cause rather than
the simple "this is how it was" of historical sequence. Thus,
while using the surface discourse of narrative, it appears to turn
itself into an allegory of intentional creation: how (that is,
why) he *had to* write *La Celestina*. In the early version, he says
that the initial fragment was without signature: in the *Tragicomedia* he adds that some attribute it to Juan de Mena, others
to Rodrigo Cota. In the introductory verses, meanwhile, the same
explanation is offered for the genesis of *Celestina* with the
difference that in the *Tragicomedia* the attribution to "Cota or
Mena" is given as certainty, not what "some" or "others" think.

No judgment on the matter—no knowledge or hearsay, not
even an apocryphal tradition to fill the strange silence—has come
to us from Rojas' lifetime. If ever there had been knowledge
of Rojas' discovery and continuation of this fragment (or, on
the other hand, knowledge of his practical joke in fabricating an
anonymous fragment) that knowledge did not reach any other
writer. In his *Dialogo de la Lengua* (Dialogues on Our Language) written in 1535/36 Juan de Valdés gives greater praise
to the "first" author than to the "second" in the matter of wit,
but ranks them equal in judgment.[1] If this means anything more
than that the first deserves greater admiration because he is the
innovator, it is not obvious. But it is worth noting that Valdés
does not name *either* author. Rojas was still alive in 1535,
living in Talavera, in the jurisdiction of Toledo, the imperial city
where the Valdés brothers had spent years in the service of
Charles V and where *La Celestina* had been published. Yet
Valdés refers merely to "first" and "second" authors. A man and
his work were more easily separated then than they are now,
and in Spain a writer's reputation often remained in small
circles. From this point on, wherever one finds *La Celestina*

mentioned, it is without benefit of author. Cervantes did not
name an author when he wrote the verses which allude to
*Celestina.* Curiously, each of the two stanzas which compose
this poem makes reference to a work of literature: the first to
*Celestina,* the second to *Lazarillo de Tormes,* the anonymous
short picaresque novel. Did Cervantes deliberately pair these
two works not only because they were both radical innovations
but also because, as far as his generation was aware, they were
both anonymous, in humorous contrast to *Don Quijote* with its
proliferation of "authors"?

In the reader's mind, one observation easily conspires with
another. If Rojas really feared that idle tongues would scorn
his writing *Celestina* instead of attending seriously to his studies
in law (I, 6–7), why is his name then revealed in the acrostic?
And why is it Proaza who points out where to find the acrostic?
Since the game is given away already in 1500, why does Rojas'
name never appear at the front of any printed edition? What
game it is that Rojas is playing in concealing himself with one
hand and revealing himself with the other? Or does one hand,
perhaps, not belong to him at all? During the nineteenth century,
increasing attention was paid to the text and to the question
of authorship. Documentary evidence for the existence of Rojas
himself had long ago been lost and was not rediscovered until
the last third of the century. It was easy, under such conditions,
to speculate on a literary hoax in which Rojas, for whatever
reason, disclaimed act I, especially since it was also easy to
disbelieve him when he said he finished the other fifteen acts in
as many days. It might have been an act of authorial pretense,
of no particular significance. The suggestion was also made that
Rojas may have wished to conceal his authorship of so in-
decorous a work[2] (in which case, why allow his name to sneak
into the acrostic?). If, on the other hand, he really did not write
act I himself, who did? Is it really likely that such a fragment
could circulate without its author being known? Was Rojas
covering the true author by the pretense of anonymity in the
*Comedia* preliminaries, and by mentioning Cota and Mena in
the later version? It was suggested that Rojas was protecting
another author (Encina was one candidate for the position)[3]
because the work was of an improper character. If the sexual

nature of the intrigue were the matter of concern, however, it is an obvious fact that Rojas' continuation would be far more offensive than act I read separately.

## II Artistic Continuity

These questions and others like them can easily be asked, but however one answers them, one is no nearer to historical certainty. If this kind of interrogation of the text cannot yield the facts of the matter, perhaps aesthetic judgment can contribute by pointing to discontinuities of conception, unresolvable dissonances of style, and disparity of vision between the two parts which will tend to confirm Rojas' statement that he is not the only author. But here is another impasse because if, on one view, the first act is planned differently from the rest, contains a much greater range of action than the others, and is simply much longer than any other (from two to eight times as long), the reader is also impressed by the way that the dramatic possibilities of the first act are perceived and realized, the characters sustained, and the dialogue equal in its expressive range. In the words of Menéndez Pelayo,

> Rojas moves within the fiction of *La Celestina* not like one who continues another's work but as one who has his own work completely in hand. It would be the most prodigious feat of literature, not to mention psychology, for a continuator to enter so completely into another man's idea, to identify himself in such a manner with the original author. . . . we do not know of any composition in which such a feat has been achieved. . . .[4]

Such an observation carries considerable weight but cannot be conclusive. Every masterpiece is unique and, until it happens, impossible. It is realized within conditions of language, convention, historical moment, personal vision, etc., etc. never before combined. One must be cautious of saying that anything is impossible, and especially in a period when training in rhetoric encouraged mastery of styles rather than a personal style, when one of the characteristic poetic forms, the *recuesta* ("challenge"), required that a second poet respond in the verse, rhythm, rhyme, and using the same lexicon, as the first. And, if we stop to think, there are some surprisingly successful collaborations in the history of literature: Calderón with a half-dozen other playwrights, Beaumont with Fletcher; there is a serious possibility that someone else took up the work of Rabelais, in the *Fifth Book*. It should really be less surprising in the dramatic mode, since the dramatist has to be, by genius and inclination, the master of many voices, able to write in every style and to conceal his own. Late nineteenth-century postromantic scholars and critics, however, worked with a different set of assumptions. They inherited a rather exalted concept of the genius of the artist and leaned heavily on the ideas of unbounded freedom and creative originality. To a mind which is molded in that form, the suggestion that a writer could shape himself so completely to the style and purpose of another (or, more exactly, welcome the other's as his own) would seem repugnant or absurd.

## III   *The Additions*

The extended version, the *Tragicomedia* with its five additional acts and other amplifications, has also been the object of skepticism. Emphasis on "sincerity" as a value in literature in the nineteenth century, and much of the present century also, grants little freedom to the author to improvise new postures in the presence of his public. For Rojas tells us, in the *Prólogo*, that he enlarged his work at the request of friends who wanted more love scenes. Of course, he has given us more than that, but we can appreciate his declaration as a *reductio ad absurdum* by a witty writer. Many readers, however, have been unable to accept his explanation and have seen him as the innocent victim exploited by an unscrupulous hack who profited from the *Comedia*'s success. Such a view presupposes that the longer version is inferior to the shorter one. We shall examine this question later (chapter 7), but we may note for the present that preference for the earlier form fits well with another preconception, "the belief that good taste, pruning, and rigid control of language are indispensable to the making of literature."[5] Cejador, author of the most widely used modern edition, attributed the additions to Proaza and poured scorn on him in the footnotes at every opportunity.[6]

## IV   *The Search for a "Scientific" Solution*

Positivist skepticism reached an absurd extreme at the turn of the century when the French scholar R. Foulché-Delbosc supported the view that the *Tragicomedia* was inferior to the *Comedia*. Since no author would mutilate his own work, the former must have been completed by a different hand. But since act I was not by Rojas, and since the acrostics were, to his mind, unbelievable, *Celestina* is the work of two authors— neither of whom was Rojas!—one of them (the mastermind) being the "malicious" writer of the letters and verses. Rojas is his invention![7] So, we are confronted by a literary fraud of the first magnitude. This is the age of Sherlock Holmes, and Foulché-Delbosc's prejudices have led him away from objective scholarly detection into detective fiction. Skepticism can create strange fantasies to replace what it doubts. More recently, in search of objective criteria, stylistic studies have compared act I and the additions to the other fifteen original acts.[8] But, in the outcome, both personal taste and scientific inquiry produce the same variety of explanations. R. E. House's analyses of linguistic features, for example, pointed to the conclusion that there were three authors. Common experience tells us, however, that a man's habits of style and his verbal preferences (where equal alternatives are available) may change detectably in a few years. And Rojas was a young man living at a time of rapid linguistic change. So we have the curious situation that painstaking statistical verbal analyses show that Rojas was not telling the truth either when he said he *did* write the additions or when he said he did *not* write act I.[9]

## V   *Conclusion*

Since scholarly ingenuity has exhausted itself in search of explanations, perhaps we should allow common sense to make two proposals. First, since the authorship of act I cannot be established, we accept Rojas' explanation, but not too strictly. In other words, we accept the probability that he would have made some changes in what he found, as well as matching his continuation to it. As for the time taken to write it, Rojas tells us that the fragment fascinated him for some time before he began to write. The "fifteen days," then, could well be the time taken to complete the final draft. Second, we take his word that he expanded the *Comedia* into the *Tragicomedia*, and we make no assumptions about which is superior. We shall reserve artistic comparisons between the two versions for a more suitable place.

## CHAPTER 4

# Tragicomedia de Calisto y Melibea:
# *Summaries and Commentaries*

ACT I: The young Calisto encounters Melibea and addresses her with words of passionate adoration, but she repulses him. Back in his room, he is sunk in despair. He seeks consolation in solitude and music and in the advice of his servant, the cynical Sempronio, who eventually offers to secure the professional help of old Celestina. In Celestina's house, Sempronio is deceived by his paramour Elicia and then returns with Celestina to Calisto's lodging. As they wait outside, Pármeno, another servant of Calisto, gives his master an account of Celestina's activities and accomplishments—former whore, now brothel keeper, witch, repairer of broken maidenheads, peddler of cosmetics and quack medicines—but Calisto is not deterred. Opening the door, he welcomes her, and, while he goes to find money to give her, she begins to talk Pármeno out of his hostility (by holding out promises of pleasure) and to shake his fidelity to Calisto. At the end of this act Pármeno is beginning to temporize with Sempronio.

*Commentary.* This is the act which, according to the prefatory letter ("El auctor a un su amigo"), was discovered by Rojas ready-made and to which he added the acts which follow. The probability of this statement's being true and the various interpretations that can be put upon it, were discussed in the last chapter. Whatever Rojas did or did not write, we must assume that the book as a whole is his in at least one valid sense, namely, that everything which he took over is given a vital place in the development of his own conception. Calderón incorporated verses by Góngora into his play *El príncipe constante* (The Steadfast Prince) and act II of his *Absolom's Hair* is lifted from act III of Tirso de Molina's *La Venganza de Tamar* (Thamar's Revenge). In each case, the primary literary fact is that what the writer took from someone else is made to serve a new dramatic idea. It has acquired a new meaning by being deployed in a new structure. We may feel differently about a work of literature in which we know that the author has used something ready-made, not "his own," but our feelings about this are rarely helpful in trying to understand the work in question, or in assessing its coherence. Neither authors nor their public would have given importance to such feelings before the nineteenth century.

This is the longest act of the play and the most varied in all in its aspects: character, situation, dramatic pace, and tension. Let us begin with the beginning, which sets before us the central fact of the play: Calisto is in love with Melibea. A simple matter, apparently. But love, like truth, is rarely pure and never simple. Melibea rejects Calisto because he has gone beyond the bounds of propriety in talking to her of love at all. She finds him guilty of a reckless folly (*tu loco atrevimiento*, I, 33), which would seem to put her virtue in jeopardy. Yet he spoke to her in the exalted language of religious ecstasy. Later, when they are in Calisto's room, Sempronio answers this high rhetoric with contemptuous asides and with arguments which reduce love to a level of mere animal impulse. Again, the kind of love implied by these words of Calisto can scarcely be the same as that served by Celestina, the old bawd whose professional advice is sought. The first words of Calisto referred to are these:

CAL. In this, Melibea, I see the glory of God.
MEL. In what, Calisto?
CAL. In giving to Nature the power to endow you with such perfect beauty, and in granting me, though unworthy, the favor of seeing you in a favorable place where I can declare my secret passion. (I, 31–32)

But this act, which begins with Calisto praising God for his favors, ends with Calisto giving a hundred gold pieces to Celestina as the price of *her* favors. Thus it is already clear that this story of boy-meets-girl is shaping into a set of relationships (personal, social, and commercial) which are profoundly unstable. If our first inclination is to see in the union of young lovers a sign of hope and joy in the goodness of nature, our feelings are quickly diverted by a much deeper and less comforting drift of motives, desires, and evasions. We are witnessing the beginning of a dramatic train of cause and effect. It will be one object of these summaries to examine this sequence, to see how and why the author has moved events in this direction.

Calisto calls his manservant, Sempronio, whose hallmark is humbug, and who reproaches his master at length for yielding to so unworthy a thing as a woman. He cautions against women's unbridled sensuality and cunning, which, of course, simply excites Calisto even more. His contempt for women is just one aspect of his complete vulgarity. He says he knows it all from experience, though the reader can see that most of it is second-hand pulpit stuff. Having agreed to search for Celestina to help Calisto, he goes to her house (that is, her brothel), where at that moment his girl Elicia is entertaining another man in her room. In a fine bit of acid comedy she smuggles the man out with such practiced innocence that Sempronio is even forced to apologize for his jealousy (I, 63). So that is our "man of experience." Such reversals are fundamental to the dramatic technique of *La Celestina*.

A natural break comes with Sempronio's departure to go in search of Celestina, but the unity of the act (which began with Calisto's "In this I see the glory of God..." and has been punctuated by similar expressions) is emphasized by Calisto's prayer for Sempronio on his "sacred" journey:

Oh, almighty and everliving God, you who guide those who are lost, and did lead the Kings of Orient to Bethlehem following a star, guide my Sempronio, I humbly pray, that he may turn my sorrow into joy and that I, though unworthy, may attain my desire at last. (I, 59)

The extravagant absurdity of such sentiments is indicated by the characterization of Celestina by Sempronio, a few lines before, as "a crafty witch, skilled in every kind of wickedness." On the return journey he insinuates to Celestina his intention to share in whatever profit is to be got (a motive which grows in importance later): "You know, ever since I learned to trust you,

I've intended to share any good fortune with you" (I, 64):
"Calisto has need of both of us, so let's both make hay" (I, 65).
While they wait at Calisto's door, Pármeno, inside, informs his
master at greater length about Celestina, "an old painted
whore" (I, 67). Here follows a set piece in mock praise of
Celestina in which Pármeno parodies the canticle *Benedicite,
omnia opera.* All things and creatures know her and cry out
her name: "old whore." All her skills in quack medicine, her
network of informants who tell her who yearns for whom and
which girls are ready for the trade, her spells, herbs, per-
fumes, and other suggestive materials are listed at impressive
length. The variety of her activities, enumerated in a tirade which
seemingly need never end, a fabulous accumulation of objects,
techniques, and professional inside knowledge pours from the
mouth of Pármeno, not as a sober narrative, not like a trade
catalog, but with the inner compulsion of a monologue by Samuel Beckett. Calisto gives him cool thanks for this revelation:
"That's enough, Pármeno. Keep it for another time..." (I, 86).
He misreads his valet's motive as envy and so promises him a
reward equal to that he has promised Sempronio. Celestina is
not satisfied by Calisto's rapturous phrases of welcome, and,
while he goes to get a more tangible gift, she attends to Pármeno,
whose epithets she overhead. She recalls his mother—a former
associate in her trade. She impresses him with her vast experience, appeals to his adolescent sensuality and sexual curiosity,
and half promises to procure for him Areusa, a free-lance prostitute who has attracted his interest. This is the first stage of
Celestina's design to "convert" Pármeno to her side, by diminish-
ing his sense of security and his moral firmness. The honest boy
is isolated by the smug cynicism of Sempronio, a much older
man, and by the thanklessness of his master. Calisto is bent
upon nothing but his "salvation" through Celestina. He is ripe
for exploitation, and this act ends with his resounding gift to
Celestina of a hundred gold pieces.

ACT II. Sempronio praises Calisto's liberality. He is now sent
to accompany Celestina to her house. Pármeno is unable to shake
his master's deluded trust in Celestina. Calisto leaves to ride
past Melibea's house.

*Commentary.* In this brief act there is little action, but some subtle shifts and definitions are presented. The dialogue continues unbroken from act I, and the first words emphasize again Calisto's disequilibrium. He asks Sempronio if he acted well in making that extravagant down payment on Celestina's services (at the end of act I). Sempronio replies with some pompous phrases on liberality, how it is better to give than to receive, and the honor that will accrue to him. In truth, we see that reckless act as being fraught with danger for his honor. Ordered to accompany Celestina, Sempronio juggles his duty to obey and his concern for what his master might do when left on his own in his desperate state of mind:

Sir, I'd like to obey you by going, and I'd like to stay and comfort you. Your fear urges me on, and your solitary brooding holds me back. Obedience tells me to go and hurry the old woman, but how can I? Because as soon as you're on your own you start raving like a madman. . . . (I, 116)

Sempronio departs, so Calisto has Pármeno to keep him company. Now Calisto alienates Pármeno, his most faithful servant, in two ways. First, he fails even to notice his presence, and second, he makes him perform the demeaning duties of a stable boy. What Celestina's attempts to seduce Pármeno have not yet achieved, Calisto's crassness will precipitate—the destruction of the young valet's personal respect and loyalty. Pármeno is angry:

I have to suffer for being loyal. Others are wicked and get ahead, and I'm a failure because I'm honest. That's how the world is. Since traitors are called wise men and loyal men fools, I'll go with the crowd. If I'd believed Celestina with her seventy-odd years of experience, Calisto couldn't have touched me. From now on I'll know better. If he says "Let's eat," I'll agree. If he wants to pull the house down, all right with me. And if he wants to burn his possessions, I'll go fetch a light. Let him smash and destroy, break and spoil, give everything away to procuresses, I'll get my share. There's good fishing in troubled waters, as they say. I'm not going to be taken for a fool again. (I, 126)

ACT III. Sempronio tells Celestina of Calisto's impatience, and also of his own desire to work with her for a share of the profit.

Celestina explains how she is winning Pármeno over. Sempronio is again reassured of Elicia's fidelity. Celestina, left alone, calls upon Pluto to aid her in the dangerous mission ahead.

*Commentary.* This act ends with an event whose significance has been widely debated—Celestina's calling upon the devil (*alias* Pluto) for help in seducing Melibea. In view of the easy course taken by later events, is this really necessary? Does Celestina really think Pluto will come in haste to do what she asks, and that he will be intimidated by her threats?

If you do not attend with all speed, you will make me your mortal enemy: I shall strike your dark and gloomy dungeons with light and mercilessly denounce your continual lies. I shall heap harsh words on your odious name. (I, 151–52).

Are we to suppose that Pluto really intervenes, or do these magic formulas simply strengthen Celestina's morale? Celestina herself does not remember Pluto in the moment of success; she knows her own skill and the human weakness of her opponent. And indeed, these factors are dramatically sufficient. Whether Rojas, or his "average" reader (whoever that may have been) would have believed in the literal truth of this scene is difficult to discuss. The only sure thing is that the conjuring has a *literary* model: it is not a realistic scene of witchcraft (see chapter 7).

Apart from this gruesome comedy, the act consists of a prolonged conversation between Celestina and Sempronio, in which the old woman takes the measure of his eagerness to be of service. (He had seen the gold Calisto gave her at the end of act I.) She replies to his tale of Calisto's amorous impatience with the observation that lovers, in their impatience, overlook the risks to themselves, "and to their servants." Sempronio's response reveals the extent of his loyalty to Calisto. It is clear to Celestina also how little she could count on him, but she is an old hand at her trade, and she knows that her profession is a lonely one and is shrewdly alert to protestations of friendship and offers of alliance:

SEMP: What do you mean, their servants? Do you mean to say that
this affair can do us any harm, that sparks from Calisto's fire
could burn us? To the devil with his love, then! At the first
sign of any trouble in this affair I'll leave his service. I'd
rather give up my pay than lose my life collecting it. Time
will tell. There's bound to be some warning signal, like in a
house that's going to collapse. Don't you think we should
keep out of danger, Mother? Let things go their own way:
maybe he'll get her this year, maybe next, maybe never.
... Let's make the most of it while he's roused. ... Otherwise, better for the master to suffer than the servant to get
into trouble. (I, 128–29)

Celestina has allowed Sempronio's edgy cynicism to play itself
out adding only a few phrases of approval. But when he observes, with leaden banality, "Do as you like; I don't suppose
this is the first affair you've taken on" (I, 133), she is provoked
into proclaiming her professional record:

The first, son! You haven't seen many virgins set up shop in this city,
thank God, whose goods I haven't been the first to push. The moment
the girl's born I write her down in my book, so I know how many
escape my net. ... (I, 133)

The movement is subtle. Sempronio has been trying to insinuate
himself as Celestina's equal in worldly wisdom, to qualify as
her companion and so to share in the spoils. Having provoked
the sudden assertion of her undisputed authority, he rapidly
changes the subject to Pármeno and asks what passed between
her and him. This is a shrewd psychological move by Rojas, who
has the uneasy and outwitted Sempronio turn the conversation
to the one person to whom he feels superior. He is hoping to be
taken into her confidence after the unfortunate reminder of his
inferiority. But what she tells him of Pármeno is that she and
his mother were inseparable, like sisters; that in order to win
him over she has promised him the pretty Areusa. All this must
have set Sempronio's teeth on edge, for when the talk comes
round to Melibea once more, Sempronio's spirits have fallen.
He began this act querulous at Celestina's mention of danger:
now he anticipates the terrors of the enterprise:

Look what you're doing, Mother, because if you make a bad start, you'll come to grief. Think of her father, who's brave and noble, and her mother who's fiercely jealous, and you—you'd arouse anyone's suspicions. (I, 140)

And again, his fear reveals his motive: "I want to get something out of this affair, I want it to end well. Not to get my master out of his grief, but to get myself out of poverty" (I, 141). Act III is a fine example of Rojas' capacity to dramatize fully. It has the theatrical invocation of the devil by Celestina, solo. It has conversations which change direction in obedience to the characters' anxieties. It reveals, as apparent and momentary irrelevances, remote desires which will converge inexorably upon the catastrophe.

ACT IV. On the way to Melibea's house, Celestina debates with herself the dangers and difficulties of her mission. At the house she assumes her role of peddler, is recognized by the servant Lucrecia and by Melibea's mother, and finally is left alone with Melibea. At the first indication of the reason for the visit, Melibea becomes very angry, but Celestina pretends to have been misunderstood. She explains that Calisto is ill. To recover he needs the aid of a prayer, and also he must touch a pious relic—Melibea's *cordón* (the knotted belt or girdle which she wears round her waist). Melibea drops her harsh manner and agrees that Celestina may return to complete the errand another day.

*Commentary.* In act I, Sempronio had debated with himself about whether to enter Calisto's room and offer help, or to leave him alone. That debate between two arguments from self-interest was never settled because Calisto called Sempronio into his presence. By contrast, Celestina carries her debate forward to a conclusion. The dilemma is put in these terms: if she is discovered, her soliciting could cost her her life or, at the least, a public whipping. But if she does not go on, Sempronio will think she is a fraud (since she argued so convincingly against his fears), and Calisto will either suspect her of betraying him or turn violent in his frustration. Her conclusion is: "I'd rather offend Pleberio than make Calisto angry. I'll go,

for the shame of holding back like a coward is greater than the
punishment I might get for boldly keeping my promise..."
(I, 156). She argues like a soldier facing enemy fire. And like
the soldier, she argues less from courage as a moral quality than
from professional reputation. She vividly imagines (I, 155)
Calisto's angry tirade at length; on the other hand she does not
compose Pleberio's possible vengeance in her mind. In other
words, her powers of rhetoric are selectively employed, and she
represents to herself only that danger which is a threat to her
professional pride. In doing so, she undoubtedly does screw up
her courage, since the fury of outraged respectability is not
something to be risked lightly. Her morale is supported, on this
occasion, by superstitious omens, not by aid of Pluto:

The omens are all favorable, or I know nothing of the matter. Four
men I've passed and three of them are called John, and two of them
cuckolds. The first word I heard on the street was about love. I
haven't stumbled like other times. Not a dog has barked at me, I've
not seen any black bird, no crow or raven or other night birds. . . .
(I, 157–58)

Favorable omens merge into the favorable disposition of events:
". . . But the best thing is that I can see Lucrecia at Melibea's
door. She's Elicia's cousin and won't work against me" (I, 158).
Celestina's arrival brings into relief some strange contrasts (prim
servant, lax mother) in Melibea's household. Lucrecia can
scarcely bring herself to name Celestina and takes the round-
about way of naming all her trades. When finally she utters
the terrible name ("begging your pardon, madam"), Alisa bursts
out laughing and orders Celestina to be shown in. With what
may perhaps be a foolish display of superior broad-mindedness
intended to impress the young, Alisa reveals the first weakness
in the moral fabric of the household. The defensive hostility
which Celestina had expected to meet, the protective caution
which she knew would be proper to such a household, has dissolved into frivolous mirth at Lucrecia's discomfort: "He, he he!
a pox on you if I can stop laughing! How you must hate the old
woman if you're even shamed to mention her name. . . ." Alisa,
in her own way, repeats Calisto's offense, the treason of the
master against the loyalty and trust of the servant. To Celestina's

amazement, again, Alisa leaves her with Melibea so as to go
visiting.

Alone with Melibea, Celestina shows her true professionalism.
Whatever she may feel privately about her old age, she deploys
it skillfully. Not, of course, to arouse sympathy for her pains,
her poverty, or her departed charms, but to make Melibea aware
of time even now robbing her of youth. She prepares her ground
further by emphasizing that she is not soliciting help for herself but for another, one who is sick, one whom Melibea can
help out of the nobility of her heart, and so on. By a combination of flattery, piety, and provocative hesitation, Celestina brings
Melibea to the point of wanting to know what Celestina wants
to tell her. But the mention of Calisto's name, when it comes,
causes Melibea to explode in a passion of fury:

> . . . .I'll see you burned, you wicked deceitful bawd, you witch, you
> enemy of virtue, you provoker of secret sins! Sweet Jesus! Get her
> out of my sight, Lucrecia. . . . It's only out of regard for my reputa-
> tion and because I don't want to make the villain's effrontery public
> that I don't put an end to that talk and your life right now. (I, 178)

For all her angry words, Melibea does not throw Celestina out.
Instead, she continues to insult Calisto and, strangely, to ask
Celestina what excuse she can find for her conduct. The old
woman knows that the danger is past; she says Calisto has a
toothache and that it can be eased by her rope belt, which,
people say, has touched every holy relic in Rome and Jerusalem.
When Melibea hears this, she cries, "Why didn't you say so
before? And why did you come out with it so abruptly?" (I,
182). The strangeness of Melibea's questions (Celestina, far
from being abrupt, has proceeded by wily indirection) show
that she is deeply perturbed. Celestina has clearly seen into
the nature of this perturbation more clearly than the reader or
than Melibea herself. Disarmed and put off balance by Celestina's seemingly charitable motive and innocence of manner,
she does not object as the old woman slyly praises Calisto, his
charms, his youth, his accomplishments. Finally, Melibea relents:

> O, how I regret losing my temper! He all unknowing and you in your
> innocence have suffered the lash of my angry tongue. But your

suspicious way of talking did give me cause. To repay your patience
I'm going to give you my belt right away, as you asked. And since
there won't be time to write down the prayer before my mother
returns, come back for it tomorrow secretly if the belt isn't enough.
(I, 188–89)

Lucrecia, in the wings, observes: "O, my mistress is ruined!
She wants Celestina to come in secret, does she? There's some
shady business; she'll end up giving more than she said" (I, 189).
Lucrecia judges by what she knows of Celestina's ability and
reputation, and Melibea's imprudence. The reader, his eye
sharpened by hindsight, may see something more in a phrase
Melibea spoke before her angry outburst: "How fortunate I am
if any Christian's health depends on a word from me! To do
good is to be like God, what you give you get back if the
receiver is worthy" (I, 175). It is almost as if Melibea saw herself in the mirror of Calisto's adoration of her; an adoration,
we remember, which was clothed in the rhetoric of religious
fervor.

To return to Lucrecia, Celestina catches, if not her very
words, certainly the tone and intent of her recalcitrant muttering. So she tempts the girl through her vanity, as she had
tempted Pármeno through his youthful sensuality into disloyalty
and into sacrificing his moral independence.

Hush, Lucrecia, dear! Come to my house and I'll give you a lotion
that'll make your hair brighter than gold. Don't tell your mistress.
And I'll give you some powder, too, that will cure your bad breath—
there's nothing worse in a woman—and no one else in the whole kingdom knows how to do it. (I, 190)

She also advances her ground with Melibea before she leaves:

Even supposing I said what you thought I did, there was nothing
wrong in it. Every day men suffer for women, and women for men;
that's how Nature works, and Nature was ordained by God, and
God made nothing evil. (I, 191)

Celestina has come through her most trying time, she has Melibea's permission to return next day, and she has left with Melibea

a set of insidiously naturalistic propositions, which the girl did not attempt to contradict. Strategically, she has established a convenient fiction (physical pain) within which she can name Calisto, a metaphor which at any moment could be displaced by the erotic reality which it is disguising.

ACT V. Celestina leaves Melibea's house in a state of elation and returns to her lodging where Sempronio awaits her news. Together they go to inform Calisto, talking along the way.

*Commentary.* It is a brief act but full of interest and extraordinarily varied within its short span. Celestina rejoices on the road, addressing herself, her powers, her potions, her past anxieties, her present good fortune. Sempronio is greedy for her news, but she reserves it for Calisto and, in the same thought, lets slip a small phrase which will have profound consequences.

CEL.      I want him to know from my own lips what has happened. For although you may get a little bit of the profit, I want all the thanks for my labor.

SEMP.      A *little* bit, Celestina? I don't like the sound of that.

CEL.      Quiet, you silly! A bit, or a little bit, I'll give you whatever you want.... (I, 196–97)

Celestina has won over the servants by hinting at the profit to be got from his passion. The danger to herself of this appetite, once it is aroused, is already threatening. She makes some conciliatory phrases but leans heavily on the necessities of age.

CEL.      Think, Sempronio, how hard it is to keep up appearances when you're getting old, as I am.

SEMP.      (*Aside*) You false old devil, you wicked old woman! You grasping greedy-guts! So you want to cheat me the way you've cheated my master, just to make yourself rich. Much good it'll do ... I wouldn't want to be in her shoes.... (I, 198)

Next, he questions her tactics in telling Calisto of her success; the longer the affair is drawn out, the greater the profit to be earned.

Meanwhile, Calisto is advised by Pármeno of Celestina's arrival. His delirious exclamations ("Oh great God, oh, sovereign deity!... Oh ... Oh...," I, 200–201) echo and balance those with which Celestina began this act. As the servants hover for the prey, Celestina and Calisto begin to establish a new formal balance of mutual interests within the plot.

ACT VI. Celestina reports to Calisto on the progress she has made while Sempronio and Pármeno observe how she angles for another reward. When she produces Melibea's belt, Calisto becomes delirious with joy.

*Commentary.* The act is intense with contrary motives and feelings. Calisto trembles in suspense, while Celestina gasps for breath and dramatizes the dangers she has just come through ("I'd have given less for my life than this old cloak is worth...." I, 204) and insinuates her desire for a reward. Pármeno, only recently recruited by Celestina, still looks with bitter anger at her mercenary greed and Calisto's abject capitulation. His own greed, newly awakened to replace his loyalty to Calisto, oscillates violently:

Don't miss a word she says, Sempronio, and you'll see she doesn't ask for money because that can be shared. (I, 204)

The old whore wants to make up in one day and three steps what she didn't make in fifty years. (I, 205)

Sempronio, who restrains Pármeno's criticisms of Celestina's thirst for money, loses his patience with Calisto's lack of control as the old woman tells of her encounter with Melibea.

PARM. And you tell *me* to shut up, Sempronio! If the master hears, he'll as likely punish you as me.

SEMP. Oh, go burn in hell! *Your* talk is against all our interests but I don't hurt anyone. May you die of a horrible plague, you damned envious troublemaker! Is this the pact of friendship you entered into with Celestina and me? Clear out of here, and bad luck to you! (I, 207)

Next, Calisto addresses the kind of passionate discourse to Celestina that he would if she were Melibea,

If, my queen and lady, you do not wish me to despair and send my soul to everlasting torment, tell me straight away whether your glorious mission was successful; whether the cruel and ruthless expression on that angelic and death-dealing countenance was more favorable.. . . (I, 207)

Celestina who, as we have seen, faced Melibea full of apprehension and uncertainty, improvising her part as she went along and having a great deal of help from luck, now plays upon Calisto. She fully makes up for her previous hesitancy by demonstrating her control of him, arousing his fears that his love is doomed, then raising his hopes to the pitch of ecstasy. In fact it is one of the many ironies of this book that Celestina's art (her purposeful manipulation of human material) is far more effective with the abject Calisto than with the spirited Melibea. And Celestina cannot at this moment resist the satisfaction of her spectacularly cheap victory over him. And Calisto, while he celebrates her supremacy in her craft ("What marvelous cunning! Without compare in your profession! Crafty woman! And such a swift remedy! . . ." I, 215) celebrates without knowing the guile with which she has played upon his feelings and his purse strings. The climax of her performance is to produce Melibea's belt, which he then treats as a fetish or holy relic. "Oh blessed girdle, to have been given the power and made fit to encircle the body which I am unworthy to serve! In your knots my passion and all my desires are caught. . ." (I, 220). He fondles it, addresses it and questions it with such abandon that Celestina becomes impatient: "Enough of this raving, sir; I'm as tired of hearing you as the belt is of being mauled" (I, 222). Sempronio even raises his usually servile voice against the impropriety: "Sir, you're so worked up with the belt that you won't want to enjoy Melibea" (I, 223). Finally Celestina tries to bring him back to reality: ". . . stop these complaints and treat the belt like a belt. . . . don't speak to the person and the garment as if they were the same" (I, 224).

Calisto imagines all women hopelessly envying and trying to rival the beauty of Melibea, while Celestina and the servants

make sarcastic asides. When the old woman has to leave, saying that she needs the belt, Calisto is once more thrown into
dismay: "Oh, how wretched I am, ill luck is never far behind
me! If only I could have had the girdle or you, or both to keep
me company this long dark night . . ." (I, 228). Calisto continues
absorbed in the rhetoric of passion: suffering is hopeless, his
loved one distant and cruel, her attributes divine, but she refuses
mercy to her worshipper.

ACT VII. Celestina urges Pármeno to be more friendly with
Sempronio, in the interests of everyone. She appeals to the
memory of his mother, and he reminds her of her promise to
obtain Areusa for him. This she does; Pármeno spends the night
with Areusa, and Celestina returns home, where she is met by
the reproaches of Elicia.

*Commentary.* Celestina continues her efforts to corrupt young
Pármeno. They are successful, of course, because it is all done
with kindness, with a tear or two in pious recollection of his
mother, and with an appeal to the good of the group and its
enterprise. As we would expect, the word which comes most
readily to her lips is *love*: "my love for you." She speaks nothing
but good about him; he is like a son to her. How sad that he
should repay her by muttering, and backsliding instead of heed-
ing her sound advice! The vocabulary of love is interlaced with
that of commerce. There is, as we know, a kind of parental
righteousness which insists upon gratitude, upon what is "owed,"
and Celestina is able skillfully to exploit this vein of moral
coercion. Her first words, "Pármeno, my son, . . ." set the key of
this discourse.

On Pármeno's side is his need for identity as an orphan in
an uncertain world, his precarious status as servant, his profound dilemma (which is present in any life of service, whether
domestic, political, or any other) of having to recognize and
choose between the master's enduring good and his passing
whim or pleasure. But before he can choose, he must recognize
that the dilemma exists, and to recognize it implies a moral
perceptiveness which many servants would be content not to
possess or cultivate, preferring rather to move from one moment

to the next, do as they're told, and let the master look after his
own good name. Sempronio has long ago settled for the philosophy of accommodation: keep the master happy and stay in
favor. Pármeno has from the first been quick to perceive the
shabby aspect of everything which is happening around him
and equally ready to comment audibly. He has not yet lost the
sharp child's view of what the adult world ought to be like.
Such an attitude rocks the boat in which Celestina is steering
Calisto to his pleasure and her own profit. Pármeno has to be
taught to play for favors as others do and not to interfere with
his elders and betters. Since he is bright and honest, and naturally inclined to respect, Celestina's purpose is to confuse him
with morality and with reverence for the better judgment of his
superiors. Seducing him through his desire for Areusa is but one
aspect of this exploitation of gratitude, one more perversion by
Celestina of the role of mother and provider for her child.

Pármeno, my son ... I've not had time to show how much love I
bear you.... I always thought of you as a son and expected that
you would behave like one, and you repay me by contradicting me
to my face.... After listening to my good advice I didn't expect to
find you backsliding ... you speak what comes into your head instead
of what stands to reason.... good counsel belongs to your elders,
and pleasure to the young.... You need to put by for old age....
Now look at Sempronio.... (I, 231–34)

The thread of her argument is unmistakable: "Don't be foolish,
learn from my experience, and it's all for your best interest as I
have been a second mother to you." The parental style, the blend
of emotional appeal and moral command, the indulgent "I can't
be angry with you because you're too young to know any better," the devious resort to "wisdom" as commonly exercised by
spokesmen for practicality ("Stop preaching and let's all get
on with the job") is calculated to trap and confuse. The familiar
topics, the hallowed imperatives of filial behavior, are used to
present a world which inverts the values which Pármeno has
intuitively grasped. Acts of brainwashing, as we know from the
many examples in recent history, are not complete without an
act of confession, and Celestina's conversion of Pármeno follows
the pattern: "Mother, I confess I have done wrong, and I beg

you to forgive what is past and to advise me for the future"
(I, 234).

It is clear, however, that the victory is not the work of Celestina alone. She has exploited the loneliness and isolation caused
in Pármeno by Calisto's selfish disregard of the boy's concern
for him. With his characteristic impetuous honesty, he lets it
out: "I'm sorry I said what I did. I said it not so much because
I disapproved what you were doing but because I saw that when
I gave him [Calisto] good advice I got no thanks for it" (I, 237).
Where Pármeno has offered his true self and been rejected,
Celestina comes in with spurious and alluring images of love and
gratitude.

In extending her protectiveness to Pármeno, Celestina pro-
nounces a eulogy of his mother, celebrating their close friendship and professional association. His mother, like Celestina, was
a witch, procuress, and midwife, and she suffered public
punishment.

You know, the devils themselves were afraid of her, she had them
terrified with her bloodcurdling screams. She was as much at home
with them as you are in your own house. They came tumbling over
one another when she called. . . . (I, 241)

Next, Celestina briefly insinuates that there is a legacy to be
inherited from his father. Then, from the dead mother and
father, by a beautiful psychological insight, Rojas has Pármeno's
mind suddenly shift to the living, the tempting Areusa. He has
desired her but never succeeded in approaching her. Celestina
wastes no time in taking him to the girl's house and overriding
Areusa's objections. Again, Celestina's persuasions employ
images of trade: "Don't be stingy with something which didn't
cost you anything. Don't hoard your charms, it's only right they
should circulate like money, so don't be the dog in the manger"
(I, 250). She does not leave until she has got Pármeno into
Areusa's bed and enjoyed watching some of the sport: "I'm going
now; you're making my mouth water with all your kissing and
playing. I still have the taste in my gums; it didn't leave me when
my teeth fell out" (I, 260). Back at her hovel, Celestina is met
by Elicia who reminds her of all the clients she has been ne-

glecting. There are broken maidenheads to be restored, work which Elicia detests (I, 261–62). For a moment we see her frustrated desire for independence; she is trapped in enjoying the pleasures of the day but has no taste for those skills of cunning and fraudulent art with which Celestina ekes out her old age.

ACT VIII. The next morning Pármeno leaves Areusa and returns late to Calisto's house. Sempronio is waiting, and they now enter into friendship. A supper is arranged for Celestina's house that night. They wake Calisto who then goes to church where he will await news from Celestina.

*Commentary.* "Now I've really let my master down badly" (II, 7). It is midday as Pármeno wakes up in bed with Areusa. The faithful servant has betrayed his trust. This is what Celestina wanted: loyalty to be replaced by self-indulgence. Overjoyed with his first night of lovemaking, he now needs to share his pleasure verbally, in friendship. The only candidate for his confidences, of course, is Sempronio, so they become reconciled. Again, Celestina's design has been fulfilled. Theirs is not the friendship as defined by moralists (by Cicero's authoritative *On Friendship* or Boethius' *The Consolation of Philosophy,* for example) but a shared complicity in which violent antagonisms are masked by expediency. Sempronio's response when he hears from Pármeno that he is in love—he who has been so scornful of Calisto's love—is:

I've heard you giving Calisto a lot of foolish advice and contradicting Celestina in everything she says and refusing to join in so as to stop her and me from getting anything out of it. Well, now I've got you where I want you and I'll squeeze you where it hurts. (II, 11)

Again, Pármeno renounces his past conduct, as he did to Celestina earlier. Sempronio is convinced of Pármeno's new change of heart when he includes him in the invitation to dine at Celestina's. He rejoices "Wonderful! That's really generous of you" (II, 15), and it is obvious who will pay: "Let's eat and be merry and let our master do the fasting for all of us!" (II, 16). They prepare then to raid the pantry for the feast where, in Pármeno's words, "We'll talk over how to turn his love affair to his loss and our profit" (II, 17).

Meanwhile, Calisto also has slept late in his chamber, with the shutters closed against the light, and singing melancholy verses. He does not know whether it is time to sleep or to get up. "Forget Melibea for a moment, sir, and you'll see the light," comments the sententious Sempronio (II, 19), and again, "What are your wits for, if your desire gets the better of your reason?" (II, 21). Before leaving the house, Calisto eats a little candied fruit. The act ends with Pármeno's coarse outburst: "The devil go with you, now and ever after! May the fruit do you as much good as the poison did to Apuleius when it turned him into an ass!" (II, 23). Pármeno's "conversion" is complete. This is clearly an event of great importance in the structure of the work, since it is achieved at the halfway point of the original version in sixteen acts.

ACT IX. At Celestina's house, the meal is disturbed by Elicia's dispute with Sempronio over the question of whether Melibea is or is not beautiful. Elicia and Areusa paint an exaggerated picture of ugliness. Celestina restores peace. Lucrecia, who is Melibea's maid and also Elicia's cousin, comes with a message from Melibea telling Celestina to come quickly and bring the belt.

*Commentary.* Now that Pármeno is no longer opposing the design to make the greatest profit from Calisto's infatuation, Sempronio is free to speak ill of Celestina. It is interesting to note here that it is Pármeno who is the more understanding and charitable toward her:

SEMP. Who the devil taught her to be so crooked?
PARM. Need, poverty, hunger. There's no better teacher in the
    world. . . . (II, 26–27)

We think of a meal as an occasion for civility and harmony, communion and trust. Here the meal hardly begin when Elicia picks a quarrel with Sempronio (II, 28); Celestina creates a peaceable interlude with her praise of wine, but Sempronio's innocent reference to "the charming and gentle Melibea" brings a long and bitter scolding from Elicia and Areusa, a torrent of pent-up resentment of the poor for the rich, the rejected for the respectable, the socially inferior for the powerful. There is resentment, too, of the prostitute for her lover. Again it is Celestina who makes peace, by encouraging them to think of love, and to start petting at the table. At this point Lucrecia arrives. The quarrel reemerges in a new mode, for, while Lucrecia is kept waiting outside the door, Areusa exaggerates satirically the hard life of a maid-servant ever at her mistress's whim, comparing it to the freedom of the low life. The representative of Melibea is thus punished, taunted, and tantalized at the same time. When she has been admitted into the room she hears Celestina reminiscing about the good times—when she was in the prime of her years and the peak of her trade—the commerce of pleasure for the whole city and every social level, and the rewards and abundance of every luxury she enjoyed. Her elegy ends, "I don't know how I can live now when I've fallen from such greatness," and she has to be comforted by the others. Lamentation for the fall from good fortune is not confined to Pleberio (act XXI). The pathos of age and changing times is as worthy of record as the sudden calamity. Lucrecia, for her part, has been so absorbed, listening in curiosity, that she has forgotten her errand. We shall see more instances of Lucrecia's vicarious enjoyment of the sensual experiences of others.

ACT X. Melibea, alone, is prey to the anguish of her secret love for Calisto and the fear of dishonor. In the presence of Celestina she resumes her scolding manner whenever Calisto's name is mentioned, but finally confesses her anguish, to which Celestina puts the name "love." Melibea agrees to receive him at the porch at midnight. Celestina leaves a few moments before the return of Melibea's mother, Alisa.

*Commentary.* Here Melibea's love for Calisto is disclosed. This act is psychologically rich and technically of an extraordinary brilliance. Melibea who, we must remember, is young, sheltered from the outside world, and has never experienced any amorous impulse, is puzzled, alarmed, and fearful of the strange new feelings that she discovers in herself. The dialogue, then, discloses these feelings, fearful and compelling, not only to Celestina and to the reader, but to herself. She is suddenly alert also to the tactics of self-esteem. Wouldn't it have been better to go along with Celestina the first time than be summoning her now and be forced to make a declaration? (II, 50). And would not it be better if women were allowed to say what is in their minds, as men do? (II, 51). The social pressures on the modality of love are easily discerned.

Celestina's action is not to plant love in Melibea, but to be midwife to it. This metaphor, however, does not take us very far. True, Celestina uses a medical analogy (since Melibea speaks of her unknown malady), and asks where the pain is, how it comes and goes, what feelings accompany it, and so on. All of this is devised in order to make it easier for Melibea to respond by hints and indirections. But Celestina knows that so strong are the social and psychic restraints on Melibea that she must proceed cautiously; but besides caution, delay has the powerful consequence of containing the pressure of emotions in Melibea, of increasing her desire for release to the point where she is unable to resist. This is a profound moment in the play, when she discovers, or allows Celestina to tell her, that she loves, and that the man she loves is Calisto whose name she refused to have spoken in her hearing. The old bawd has achieved her design, her craft has directed words to their object, but it is Melibea that we observe. It is Melibea who has suddenly came of age by accepting the word "love" and joining it to the name "Calisto." Celestina has merely satisfied one more client, but Melibea has changed from a child to a woman, and there are no reassuring rites of passage to sustain her. She is alone, in a world which has all at once become frighteningly strange and problematic. She faints momentarily (II, 60); when she recovers consciousness, it is into a new awareness of herself.

CEL.    . . . I think my stitches are giving way.
MEL.    It's my honor and my modesty that are breaking, and my sense of shame has gone weak. They were so much a part of me that they could not lightly abandon my face without taking, for a moment, my color and my strength, my speech, and most of my senses. (II, 61)

Like Pármeno, she is full of contrition for past "offenses" against
Celestina and begs her forgiveness as she confesses her passion
for Calisto. Her feelings are more truly perceived and more
authentic than when she was denying herself. But in her situation this self-perception and this efflorescence are bought at
tragically high cost: the cost of betraying the values which, a
brief moment ago, wove her into the fabric of family and society, and the rejection of reality implied in her acceptance of
Celestina as "wise and honored lady," "Mother" (II, 52), "friend"
(II, 54), "beloved mistress" (II, 57).

The return of Melibea's mother Alisa occupies only a few
lines but is more than merely a formal closure for the act. As
she leaves the house Celestina tells her that she has brought
some yarn that ran short the day before. Melibea, however,
tells her mother that she brought some cosmetic. Alisa comments,

She thought I would object to her being here, so she lied. Beware of
her, daughter, she's a cheat . . . if she comes back when I'm not here,
don't you make her welcome or look pleased. She won't come back
again if she hears virtue in your reply, because real virtue is more
fearful than a sword. (II, 65)

"Too late," as Lucrecia remarks, aside. The mother's long absence
before the return and her futile advice stress how remote she
is from her daughter.

ACT XI. Celestina catches up with Calisto as Pármeno and
Sempronio are fetching him from church and tells him that
Melibea is now his. He rewards her with a gold chain. Return-
ing to her home, she is warned by Elicia against staying out late.

*Commentary.* As Calisto's passion for Melibea moves toward its
satisfaction, so the other principal motive—the greed in Celestina and in the male servants—comes more sharply into view.
First, however, Celestina reports her success, which provokes
in Calisto a repetition of his language of religious ecstasy.

CEL. She belongs more to you than to herself.
CAL. Mind your words, Mother, and don't say such a thing, or
these boys will think you're crazy. Melibea is my lady!
Melibea is my God! Melibea is my life! I'm her captive and her
slave. (II, 68)

And when she further reports the assignation which is arranged
for midnight, Calisto exclaims, "... I can't bear such great glory,
I don't deserve so great a favor, I'm unworthy to speak to so
great a lady, and at her request" (II, 71). The two servants fear
a trap and Calisto rebukes them, "Shut up you fools, you suspicious rogues! Do you really want me to believe angels can do
wrong? For Melibea is an angel in disguise come to live among
us!" (II, 78).

In contrast to this wild idealization, the servants urge Celestina to get her reward and to press Calisto to make it a large
one. They are impatient for their share, but there is little sign
that Celestina will hurry to distribute the profits. As to the possibility of a trap, Sempronio remarks to his companion, "Just
listen to him, Pármeno. Don't worry. If there's any double-
crossing he'll pay for it. We've got good legs." (II, 73).

With this intensification of the negative themes (those which,
like fraud or greed, normally lead to disappointment, violence
and destruction), Elicia's words to Celestina sound like something more than simple prudence. They have the ring of prophecy: "What kept you so late? You shouldn't stay out like this
at your age. You'll trip and fall and kill yourself" (II, 74). The
accumulation of such dramatic ironies can only be mentioned
here; we shall treat the matter more fully in another part of
this book (chapter 7).

ACT XII. As midnight approaches, Calisto goes to his meeting
with Melibea, accompanied by the two menservants. Melibea
first says she invited him only so that she can tell him to desist
but quickly drops this pretense. Tomorrow she will admit him
to her garden. Sempronio and Pármeno, who have been ready
to flee at the least danger, now boast of their courage on the
way home. Leaving Calisto in his room, the two servants go to
Celestina and demand their share of the spoils. Celestina resists,
they grow angry, and Sempronio attacks her with his sword.
Elicia calls for the night watch, who arrive as the two men
throw themselves from the window, and Celestina dies.

*Commentary.* As the lovers move closer together, the servants
place cowardice and deceit between themselves and their master.

The night is dark, and they are well armed, but Pármeno confides in Sempronio that he has put on his lightest shoes and breeches, in order to be able to run faster. He would not have told him this if Sempronio had not first advised that they be ready to flee. Shame would have kept him in check. Shame, as we see, is closely related to morale, to one's self-image, and to the continuity of values in the individual and the group. Loss of shame, and the effects of this, is one important perspective from which we may appreciate the action of this play, since it concerns all the principal characters. Notice what happens when the men arrive at Melibea's house. Calisto tells Pármeno to go ahead and see whether Melibea has yet made her appearance at the door. The servant replies that Calisto should go: Melibea might think she has been tricked if a different man appears, or might fear that her dishonor has been made public. These are, in fact, good and compelling reasons, and Pármeno would probably have given them even if his former, uncorrupted self were speaking. Now, however, he cannot contain his joy because he has given a convincing reason to justify an ignoble feeling. The evidence of a corrupted reason is in the corrupt reasons that it gives. He leaps in the air and congratulates himself and babbles on like a child who has just learned a new trick—as indeed he has: "I'm just crazy with joy! You saw how I made him think it was in his interest that I didn't go, and it was for my own safety! Nobody can look after number one like I can!" (II, 79–80).

Just as reasons are degraded by being turned into pretexts, so feelings change their value. Private fear, contained and concealed in the face of a greater fear—public shame—becomes a source of courage. When fear is not afraid to show itself and act in public, perhaps because the system of loyalties is no longer respected, we call the result cowardice. This is the case with Pármeno whose loyalties have, as we have seen, been shattered. If only for this new companionship, Sempronio says, Celestina is to be thanked. Pármeno adds:

It's obvious that if we were embarrassed with each other we'd do anything to avoid the hateful word "coward," even to the point of getting killed here with our master, though he's the only one who deserves it. (II, 81)

The Spanish phrase that I have had to translate as "embarrassed" (*con vergüenza*) really means "having shame."

Melibea, having satisfied formality, and having put Calisto's sincerity to the briefest of tests by feigning anger, tells him to dry his tears, for she is entirely his. Her desire now is as great as was her fury when the play began:

> ...I beg you to command and dispose of my person as you will. These doors stand between us and our delight; I curse them and their powerful locks, and my weakness. But for them you would have no complaint, and I would be satisfied. (II, 86)

Calisto offers to command his servants to break down the doors but is restrained by Melibea's alarm. Fear mounts in the valets, who magnify the ferocity of Pleberio's servants, and they stand poised to run and abandon their weapons at the slightest sound. Ironically, Calisto assures Melibea that his men are a match for any opponent. So the tragicomedy of misplaced trust invades the action on a new level. The lovers separate, on the approach of the watch, having resolved to meet in her garden tomorrow night. At this point, Melibea's parents wake, disturbed by the noise, but she is easily able to explain it away.

Acts IX, X, XI, as the reader has probably observed, have followed a similar pattern. A lengthy discourse is closed by a shift of direction shortly before the end. In act IX, the arrival of Lucrecia causes the dialogue to acquire a new dimension of malice. Act X, in which Celestina at length prevails upon Melibea, ends with the return and brief comments of Alisa loaded with dramatic irony. In act XI another brief exchange of words, between Elicia, alarmed at the old woman's staying out late, and Celestina, returning after her interview with Calisto, ends the action by projecting an uncertain future upon the insistent "now" of the dialogue. At this point the series of terminal hints and warnings is reaching its climax. The reader may well expect one more omen, one more radical shift of perspective at the end. So, we are not surprised to hear Pármeno and Sempronio boast to Calisto of their valor. Then, as we assume that the recently established pattern is complete, Rojas delivers his shock. This act has not one short coda, but two. The walk to

Calisto's lodging, a purely formal return, it appears, and a comic prolongation of the theme of the valets' cowardly boasting, looks back rather than forward. But casually, in the hiatus of those small hours of the morning, with the adrenalin still running and nothing to do, Pármeno asks: "Where shall we go, Sempronio? To bed, or to the kitchen for a snack?" Sempronio responds: "You go where you like. Before it's light I'm going to Celestina to claim my share in that chain. The old whore; I'm not going to let her cook up some lie and swindle us out of our share" (II, 94). The valor which was so conspicuously absent outside Melibea's house is noisily displayed in threats to Celestina. She, however, is no coward and stands her ground. She calls them cowards, which might cause men of honor to desist. It is she, however, who has induced Pármeno to abandon honor, so her appeal can only hasten her end. For once, all her words, her repertory of irony, evocation of shared pleasures, ambiguous promises for the future, are of no effect.

Elicia's warning (end of act XI) that Celestina may fall and kill herself is like most real-life omens in that it only partially fits the facts. Yet even where it extends beyond events, Elicia's warning has a penumbra of significance which envelops a whole sequence of future acts. Celestina does not die by falling, but Pármeno and Sempronio do. Other destinies—Calisto's and Melibea's—await discovery.

ACT XIII. Calisto wakes, congratulates himself on Melibea's love, and gives orders that he is not to be disturbed. But he is awakened by his two remaining servants, the boys Sosia and Tristán, with news of the summary public sentence and execution of Pármeno and Sempronio and their murder of Celestina.

*Commentary.* Last night's joy secretly relished in the memory and disasters reported publicly: the thirteenth act moves from the lazy pleasures of the fantasy to panic dismay. Two facts, Melibea's love and the deaths of his servants, have to be accommodated in the mind of Calisto. Neither of these events is wholly natural or innocent, both relate to Celestina, and both affect his honor. If the fact that his servants killed Celestina leads to public knowledge of his association with the old bawd, both he and Melibea could be defamed. His own shame is what moves Calisto to immediate lamentation. Pármeno and Sempronio were already half dead when picked up by the watch, and they could not have felt anything when they were being beheaded, reports Sosia. "But I feel my honor hurt," retorts Calisto (II, 110). Elicia has told everyone of the gold chain, the motive of the murder:

I'll not dare show my face in public. Oh unlucky youths to have come to such a disastrous end. How my happiness has vanished! It's an old proverb that the higher you climb the greater your fall. I gained so much last night, and I've lost so much today. (II, 112)

Some semantic engineering is clearly required if the pursuit of love is to be continued with an easy conscience. We are tested by adversity, he says to himself. A useful moral judgment as a starting point for his reevaluation, since it enables him to be reconciled, without too much effort, to the misfortunes of others. In keeping with his exalted concept of Melibea, she is to remain the one fixed point in his universe: "Whatever evil or injury may come of it, I will not fail to obey the command of her for whose sake all this has happened" (II, 112). The rest is now easy. His wretched valets were "reckless," and "would have had to pay sooner or later." Celestina (now that he no longer needs her) was "wicked and deceitful," and "Heaven consented that she should end this way in payment for the many adulteries committed under her influence" (II, 112). Thus Rojas shows us Calisto "learning the lesson of adversity." He will stay in hiding, then pretend to return to the city, ignorant of what has happened. If that fails, he will feign madness (an additional irony, furnished by one of the interpolations).

ACT XIV. Melibea waits in her garden for Calisto, who arrives with Sosia and Tristán and enters by a ladder over the wall. Melibea urges him not to rush, lest he fall. After seducing her he leaves, promising to return each night. (Here begins the most extensive of the additions in the *Tragicomedia*; the original *Comedia* resumes in act XIX.) Back in his room, he considers his dishonor and how he is to act from now on. He will remain in his darkened room by day and visit Melibea by night.

*Commentary.* Melibea waits in her garden, impatient for Calisto's arrival. When he arrives, she is fearful that he may fall, and she wants to be quietly with him and enjoy his presence. He rushes in and is so impetuous that she protests at his rough handling and tearing of her clothes. While Sosia and Tristán comment on how easily he has put his dead servants out of mind, he takes her. The counterpoint of Calisto and Melibea inside and the comments of the two youths outside prevents the reader from romanticizing this moment. Melibea, lamenting the loss of her virginity and the honor symbolized in it, provokes this sardonic commentary:

SOSIA. I'd like to be the one listening to that blather! They all recite the same litany when it's too late and can't be mended. And that dolt Calisto is lapping it up! (II, 119)

"Honor" in a different aspect preoccupies Calisto later as he returns to his "other" life and awakes to the memory of his public shame caused by the deaths of his servants. He exclaims now against his inaction; why didn't he take revenge? Why didn't he go out and investigate, at least? Again, as in the similar situation of act XIII, he leans on fireside philosophy: the brevity of this world's pleasures. The instability of the world seems to lead his thought to the unreliability of the judge who had Pármeno and Sempronio executed: "Oh cruel judge, this is how you pay me for the bread you ate at my father's table! I thought that with your goodwill, I could kill a thousand men without fear of punishment. You false cheat, persecutor of truth, low-born villain!" (II, 124). He rants until even he is aware that he is ranting and recalls himself to reason. He reminds himself that justice has to be equal for all men and that, by not calling witnesses but by executing those caught in the act, by acting thus and not issuing public proclamation, the judge has in fact done all he could to preserve Calisto's honor. He has behaved, not like his father's dependent, but rather as a brother (II, 127). Now that his thoughts have reached so happy a conclusion, he can return to dwell upon the delights of Melibea. Addressing himself, he urges, "And since you value your life as nothing in her service, don't worry about the deaths of others, since no pain can equal the joy received" (II, 127). Calisto is an adroit moralist!

Having debased his "God" Melibea, betrayed his servants both while they were alive and after their death, and pronounced his love a worthy object for human sacrifice; having, that is to say, subverted all relationships, it is artistically fitting that he should now decide to make day night and night day: "By day I'll stay in my room, and by night in that sweet paradise, that happy garden, among those delicate plants and that cool verdure" (II, 127–28). We turn from the oppressive introspection and sensual fantasies when, at the end of this act, the dialogue moves to the servants. Sosia doubts that Calisto feels much grief for those who died and points from the window to where Elicia can be seen on the street. She is dressed in widow's weeds and weeping, and she is entering the house where Areusa lives. It is a relief to go from the dark, fantasy-filled room of Calisto to the window; a window where two young boys look out without affectation on the grief of others.

ACT XV. Areusa is quarreling with a braggart ruffian named Centurio when Elicia arrives and tells her the news of the deaths of Sempronio, Pármeno, and Celestina. Areusa offers to enlist Centurio to carry out revenge by killing Calisto, and to coax Sosia into disclosing his master's movements. She offers to share her lodging with Elicia, who declines the offer.

*Commentary.* The only new character in the additional acts is Centurio. Fraudulent in a different way from the others, this man is bombastic, strikes ferocious poses, but is an empty windbag and a coward. At the beginning of the act, Areusa is complaining that he will not do what she wants, but that he has robbed her, gambled away the horse with which she set him up, thrown away a steady job with a good master, and so on. He does not sound like the person to trust with an important task; yet it is difficult to believe that Areusa is so bad a judge of character. Perhaps she believes that this feckless cheat owes her too much to be able to refuse her and is just the person to make a cowardly assault from behind and in the dark.

The interest of this act, apart from introducing the idea of vengeance, as we have just seen, lies in its presentation from a new perspective of events which we have already seen happen. (We need not debate here whether it is likely that Areusa could still be ignorant of the deaths which took place some thirty-six hours before.) Those deaths were the culmination of processes involving deceit, treachery, and other repellent qualities. As we look at the relation of characters to events, a sense of "poetic justice" is unavoidable. Now, however, we see the two men, not as figures in a certain pattern of events (a contractual relation with their destiny in which, as Calisto observed in act XIII, "they were bound to pay sooner or later"), but as men who have been loved and are grieved for. True, Elicia mocked and deceived Sempronio (acts I, IX), and her manner of loving may displease many readers, but that does not mean her grief is a farce. Areusa was Pármeno's delight, although she was obviously not "faithful" in any conventional sense. But she casts around in her mind for a means of taking vengeance on Calisto and Melibea, who, she sees, are the original causes of all that has happened. Both girls mourn Celestina as mother, provider, protectress. The surprise in this act, then, is the revelation of the "villains" as objects of human feelings of love and affection, even respect. At the same time as he achieves this, Rojas also differentiates the two girls in their manner of grief. Elicia is still shocked and weeping, for, after all, she was witness to the murder of Celestina by her own lover, which is not an experience to be got over lightly. Areusa is seized by a paroxysm of terror as Elicia begins to inform her of the violent deaths,

AREUSA. What are you saying? Don't tell me. Don't say it, for God's sake, I'll die. (II, 135)

After the sudden, intense outburst she recovers her composure and advises Elicia to control her grief. Her pain is transformed into the hunger for revenge.

ACT XVI. Pleberio has decided that the time has come to provide a husband for Melibea. As he and Alisa discuss the matter, they are overheard by Lucrecia, who tells Melibea. The latter breaks into a passionate declaration that she will never renounce Calisto. Her parents, unaware of their daughter's love, continue their discussion. On hearing her mother praise her "innocence," Melibea sends Lucrecia to interrupt them.

*Commentary.* Another level of deceit is exposed, namely, that which Melibea is now compelled to practice on her parents. They, for their part, are only too willing to fool themselves. Alisa, as we saw in act X, notices too late what is happening around her, and gives advice when matters are no longer in her hands. In act IV she burst out laughing when Lucrecia confessed her embarrassment at naming Celestina. The distance that there is between Melibea and her parents, then, is not all of the daughter's making. But now is the occasion when Rojas can exploit it for the greatest dramatic irony, which is a necessary aspect of tragedy.

Pleberio begins with some familiar moral reflections on time, and how life flows away unobserved. They do not have many years left, and all their relatives have departed. They ought, therefore, to make provision for the inheritance of their property and the secure reputation of their daughter by getting her well married. There should be no difficulty, since she enjoys the four highest recommendations: "first, sense, modesty and virginity; second, beauty; third, noble birth and family; finally, wealth" (II, 146). Alisa is sure that whatever Pleberio decides is for the best, and that Melibea will obey "as befits her modesty and humility and the chaste ways she has kept" (II, 146).

Melibea's response, on being told by Lucrecia what she has heard, is a passionate declaration of devotion for Calisto. She (like Abelard's Héloise) would rather be his mistress than married. She will follow him anywhere in the world, even let him sell her into slavery, if that be his will.

If my parents want to enjoy me, they must let me enjoy him. They must stop thinking all that nonsense about marriage, because it's better to be a good mistress than a bad wife. They must let me enjoy my happy youth if they want to enjoy a happy old age, otherwise they'll drive me to destruction and themselves to their graves.... (II, 148)

... There's no place for ingratitude, or flattery or deception with so noble a lover. I don't want a husband, and I don't want a father or any family! (II, 150)

The dialogue passes back to Pleberio and Alisa. Pleberio's offer to let Melibea have freedom to choose from among her suitors, Alisa's opinion that she is too young and innocent to have any thought of marriage, their expressed belief that she is all that a proper young lady of her class should be, all this is made cruelly incongruous by that young lady's outburst of a moment ago. Whether the incongruity is predominantly comic or tragic will depend upon the perspective and the detachment of the reader at this point. I say *predominantly* comic or tragic because this act is both, and the reader cannot identify completely with either Melibea or her parents. Hearing the reasonable approach of the old man to the matter of choosing the husband, one may suspect that Melibea's frenzied rejection of marriage reveals in her a romantic who is in love with love and especially with secret and surreptitious love. The name of noble Calisto, after all, could hardly fail to appear on the short list of suitors. At the same time, an aged parent who carefully tries to arrange the future, but who knows so little about the present or the past as it affects his dispositions, must provoke a wry smile at least.

ACT XVII. Elicia, finding herself without visitors since the death of Celestina, resolves to lay aside mourning and dress up again. She visits Areusa, at whose house Sosia arrives shortly. Areusa flatters and entices him in order to gain information about the regularity of Calisto's visits to Melibea (see act XV). He parries her inquiries but reveals that he will visit Melibea tonight. Areusa and Elicia leave the house with the intention of visiting Centurio.

*Commentary.* While Pleberio reckons with death (his own) and plans for an orderly succession, others are living in the aftermath of the deaths of Celestina and the servants and making their several accommodations with reality. For the two lovers, little is changed. Their world excludes death in any but the figurative sense which is a mirror of their love. For Elicia and Areusa, the deaths of their lovers and of Celestina, after the momentary horror, signify both a loss and a gain. In this act Elicia, who has wept greatly, finds that she can no longer sustain public sorrow. It is bad for business in her profession, obviously, but that is not all. Elicia's natural vitality and gregariousness compel her to look outside, seek company, move things about, sweep floors, and so on. That is her kind of life, and the dynamic pattern will assert itself again. Areusa is overjoyed to welcome her; perhaps they will work more closely in the future. Already she is aware that in losing her "aunt" Celestina she has gained a new independence: "Perhaps it was good for both of us. I certainly feel that things are better than they were before. It's truly said that the dead open the eyes of the living, for some with legacies, for others, like you, with freedom" (II, 156).

Again, after enticing Sosia into his indiscretion, Areusa rejoices in the verbal skill, the carefully modulated flattery, the counterfeit emotion, by which she brought it off. This is an art that she was not aware of possessing while Celestina was alive and held sway:

What do you think of that? That's how I deal with men like him. Just let them fall into my hands, and the asses get a beating, the fools run for shame, the sensible ones get a scare, the pious ones are shocked and I make the chaste ones excited. See here, cousin, this is a different skill from Celestina's. She took me for a fool because that was the way I wanted it. (II, 162–63)

Since the departure of Celestina, other changes are observable also. The old woman looked backward. She voiced the elegy for time past and youth extinguished. Without her overwhelming presence, the world of La Celestina has been transformed into a world of the young who are living their moment, some self-absorbed, others predatory and aggressive. This world also contains Melibea's parents, who plan for the future while fate laughs in the wings.

ACT XVIII. Elicia and Areusa go to Centurio's lodging and act out their plan. Elicia plays the part of the mediator, and Areusa, making a show of resistance, finally allows herself to be reconciled on condition that Centurio will assassinate Calisto. He boasts of his abilities in the line of killing and agrees to do it. But as soon as the women have gone, he wonders how to get out of it and decides to ask his crony Traso to go in his place.

*Commentary.* This is the least interesting act of the play and Centurio, who takes a principal part in it, is the least interesting character. The contribution which this act makes to the process of the action is minimal. One can defend it by appeal to that old critical standby, "comic relief," but if such "relief" is required, one should be able to account for it in the total economy of the play's structure. The most noteworthy aspect of this act is that Areusa, who in the last act prided herself on being so smart, so able to outwit every kind of man, and who clearly has such contempt for the poor wit of Centurio, is fooled by her own trick. His cowardice, which is inseparable from his boasting, is impossible to hide from the audience. But what is visible to the audience is not apparent to the girls in the play. Again, one may reasonably question whether Centurio is a complex enough figure for the counterdeception to carry conviction.

ACT XIX. Accompanying Calisto on the road to Melibea's garden, Sosia tells Tristán of the good fortune he has had with Areusa, who declared her love for him. Tristán warns him to expect some trickery. Melibea and Lucrecia are singing as Calisto arrives, so he pauses to listen before descending from the wall. While they are enjoying their pleasure in the garden, Sosia is heard defying an attacker. Calisto goes to his defense— although the boys have scared away the interlopers (here the long interpolation begun in act XIV ends, and the original text of the *Comedia* resumes)—misses his foothold on the ladder, and falls to his death. He dies unconfessed. Tristán and Sosia carry away the body, Melibea grieves, and Lucrecia advises that she pretend to her father that she is ill.

*Commentary.* This act is rich in contrasts. In it situations are overturned and moods reversed, while certain expectations are fulfilled.

The catastrophe follows a pattern which is familiar to us in tragic drama: it comes suddenly and is apparently unnecessary on the level of material events and their causes. There was no real threat when Calisto rushed to the ladder. Similarly, in *Othello*, Desdemona's handkerchief is no evidence of infidelity. In both *La Celestina* and *Othello* the justification of the violent

end has to be sought in a longer view of the work, because
it is the culmination of a complex process and not merely the
result of a single immediate cause (see chapter 7). Again, our
play comes to its sudden destructive end just when a sustained
lyrical intensity appears to promise immunity from any harm-
ful twists of fate, and when the chain of causality appears to
have worked itself out. Once we have seen how cowardly and
ineffective Centurio is, we are not likely to take the plot against
Calisto's life very seriously. This is perhaps the best argument
for the necessity of act XVIII. The material introduced by the
*Tragicomedia* supposes an action which lasts one month longer
than the earlier *Comedia,* a month which suggests a stability
in the relations between Calisto and Melibea and an equilibrium
in the dramatic structure of events. The illusory nature of the
stability is emphasized by the ease with which that structure is
upset. This is one of the ways that the play gains from the additions (see chapter 7 for a fuller discussion of the interpolations).
    Sempronio and Pármeno were ready to run and leave Calisto
at any sniff of danger. Sosia and Tristán, on the other hand,
hold their ground. The reliability of the new pair of servants
also serves to make Calisto appear less vulnerable than he
seemed earlier. But, apart from contributing to the ironies of
the ending, the contrasts between the two pairs of servants are
interesting in themselves. Pármeno and Sosia, for instance, both
have dealings with Areusa. But whereas Areusa is an instrument in the corruption of Pármeno, and this corruption is wel-
comed by Sempronio, Sosia's foolish delight in her blandish-
ments is rebuked by Tristán. Sosia grows up in the opposite
sense from Pármeno, and Tristán is the opposite kind of ad-
viser from Sempronio. Why, asks Tristán, would Areusa, who can
attract men who have money and manners, want a stable boy
with mud on his boots? He smells the trap, gauging Areusa's
resentment against Melibea. Here is a new dramatic irony, in
which a minor character learns from experience just when a
leading one is being destroyed by his own blindness. The new
acceptance of reality in the lesser characters might conceivably
open a way for the principals, but any such hope in the reader
is bound to be frustrated. For one thing, the death of Calisto is
not the only tragic element in the play. Melibea must still be

considered, and his death forces her to face what she would
have to face in the end: her dishonor and the deception of her
parents. She chose to be his lover rather than consider him a
possible husband, and his death now make the choice irrevocable. Her final crisis is painfully near at hand.

ACT XX. Lucrecia wakens Pleberio to tell him that Melibea
is sick. Melibea tells him that the disease is in her heart. He
persuades her to take the air; she sends him to fetch musical
instruments while she climbs to the roof of the house, then
sends Lucrecia to say she has a message that she will call down
to him. So, as he listens from the foot of the tower, she confesses the whole history of her love. Now she must join Calisto
in death. After uttering expressions of sorrow for the grief
that she is visiting on her parents, she throws herself down
from the roof.

*Commentary.* Even in arranging for her death, Melibea has
to deceive her father. For the whole duration of the play, she
has not spoken to him, nor he to her except (in act XII) to
inquire what was the noise he heard coming from her room.
The reply was not the truth on that occasion. We noted earlier
(act XVI) that her parents do not know her but see in her
their idea of what such a daughter should be. Now Melibea
and her father speak face to face for the first time. At the beginning of this act, while Pleberio is still deceived as to the
nature of her malady, they are together, but this lasts only for
a brief moment, because she sends him downstairs on a false
pretext, while she continues her climb up to the roof. Thus, for
as long as they were on the same physical level, and near each
other, they were separated by darkness or walls, or by the
metaphorical walls and darkness of deceit. When Melibea tells
him the true history of her love, truth does not bring them
together but, on the contrary, sets the final seal on their alienation. She narrates it all from her height, separated from him by
elevation, by the moral distance she has put between them,
by her last act of cruelty in refusing him the opportunity to
exercise a father's pity and mercy, and by her command that

he remain silent until she has finished. She speaks, as it were, from beyond the grave, having already chosen damnation.

If you listen without tears you will hear the desperate cause of my forced but happy departure. Do not interrupt with talk or with weeping, otherwise you will be more grieved by not knowing why I am killing myself than by seeing me dead. Do not ask to know more than I choose to tell you and make no reply. (II, 195)

She is aware that she is condemning him and her mother to a lonely and grief-laden old age. Ironically, when she had feigned sickness near the beginning of the act, Pleberio reminded her that youth is the time for pleasure and joy, not care (II, 190). The last person who urged that view, it will be remembered, was Celestina. It may be that without the remote, routinely indulgent father and the featherbrained mother, Celestina's role would not be possible.

ACT XXI. Alisa comes out to learn the cause of Pleberio's cries. The rest of the act consists entirely of his lamentations for his lost daughter, his wasted life without heirs, the ruthlessness of the world and of fortune.

*Commentary.* The most varied interpretations have been placed on this act, which can scarcely be discussed except as it affects our understanding of the meaning of the play taken as a whole. For this reason, we refer the reader to chapters 7 and 8 for further discussion of this peroration by Pleberio.

## CHAPTER 5

# Genre and Antecedents

## I  The Questions

THE question arises, what kind of literary creation is *La Celestina*? As a drama, it is clearly unactable as it stands, though various adaptations for the stage have been made.[1] We find it unacceptable for the stage not only by reason of its length, but also because of the mobility of the speakers, who talk as they go from one place to another, destroying the stability of the location which we take for granted as a condition of theater. In our historical experience of the drama, we have come to assume that a play is not complete except in performance. If it cannot be performed it must be either a failure or something other than drama. How, then, do we classify Goethe's *Faust*, Shelley's *Prometheus Unbound* and *The Cenci*, Browning's various plays, Valle-Inclán's *Los cuernos de don Friolera*? Is the assumption that a play must be playable a just one? Or is the mode of performance, perhaps, not a necessary condition of drama? In the first part of this chapter I propose to examine, first, the way editors, critics, and commentators of recent times have classified *La Celestina*, and then to look briefly at some aspects of the history of genres (or literary classification), with the purpose of putting these difficulties into perspective. Later in the chapter we shall proceed to a summary examination of dramatic and narrative antecedents of Rojas' work. This will be followed by a contrastive phenomenology of drama and novel. Finally, the principal features of this contrastive inquiry will be observed in the structure of *La Celestina*.

## II  Conflicting Answers

During the last hundred years the question has been put with regularity by scholars who have dealt with *La Celestina*—that is to say, during a period of extreme positivistic, analytical, and classificatory activity in all fields of human inquiry. There has certainly been no unanimity in the answers, but a majority of those who have written on the matter appear to favor calling the work a drama. Rojas, after all, gave his child the names of drama (first "comedy," then "tragicomedy") and it is natural, when in doubt, to give the benefit of it to the author. On the other hand, it has not been generally agreed that Rojas chose the most apt term in calling *Calisto and Melibea* a "comedy" nor that the "tragicomedy" of twenty-one acts better deserves to be called "tragic" than the more stark and sudden catastrophe in sixteen acts.

It is characteristic that it was a German scholar, Ferdinand Wolf, who was the first to distinguish between the inner life of the work and its outer form.[2] In the "selection, construction and articulation of the story, epic predominates, on the whole"; in spite of the external form, however, the "fundamental tone and life" of the work and the action and catastrophe are dramatic.[3] Besides contrasting "external" and "internal" form, the one "epic" and the other "dramatic," Wolf extended the epic category to include the mode of speech of the characters, voluble and flown with rhetoric. Since *La Celestina* does not resemble any form known to the nineteenth century, Wolf proposes to regard it as hybrid, though allowing that the most vital (or "internal") part corresponds to drama.

Marcelino Menéndez Pelayo uses the term "dramatic poem" (*poema dramático*), in order to conciliate the dramatic form and its unsuitability for presentation on the stage.[4] The final verses by Alonso de Proaza contain a stanza on "How this tragicomedy is to be read" (*Dize el modo que se ha de tener leyendo esta tragicomedia*) which suggest that it is intended for reading aloud, since the reader is urged to make the most of whatever part he is reading. Secondly, Menéndez Pelayo notes the dependence of *La Celestina* on the Latin comedies of Plautus and Terence and their Renaissance imitators; not that Rojas is a mere imitator, but he aims "to enlarge and to surpass them by employing the same elements and fusing them into a new conception of love, life, and art." Everything about the work is dramatic: the technique, the situations, the characters, the logic of the action. It is not like the satirical dialogues of Lucian and the sixteenth-century humanists. Neither can it be called a novel in dialogue, because its "internal rhythm" could not be confused with that of the novel.[5] Menéndez Pelayo has here mentioned one of the solutions proposed, which we shall turn to next. His reason for including an exhaustive study of *La Celestina* in a treatise (which was originally also an anthology) of the history of the novel is that Rojas' work is best understood as a novel, but that historically it exerted an enormous influence on the development of fiction in Spain. This influence was more enduring in the novel than in the theater, where the realistic current was diverted by an idealizing tendency.[6] Although he does not argue the point at length, his conviction is unmistakable, and his basic concepts clear.

The title *dramatic novel* which some have tried to give Rojas' work seems inaccurate to us and a contradiction in terms. If it is drama, it is not a novel; if a novel it is not drama. The basis of novel and drama is one and the same: the aesthetic representation of human life. But the novel represents in the form of *narration*, and drama does so in the form of *action*. In *Celestina* all is active, nothing narrative.[7]

This distinction is one that will have to be examined more closely in a later section of this chapter.

Julio Cejador y Frauca has not been generally accepted as a scholar of solid judgment, but his edition of *La Celestina* (which we are following here), is undoubtedly the most widely read, as well as presenting the best available text, as we stated in chapter 2. What he has said in his introduction, then, has wide circulation. The "soul" of the work, in his view, is dramatic, and so are the characters, the events, the development, the dialogue. So far, we have an echo of Menéndez Pelayo. But Cejador rejects not only the description "dramatic novel" but also "dramatic poem" which his predecessor and mentor had used. It is not a dramatic poem because a poem is also narration (!); it is "pure drama," and as such, unperformable (I, xxxviii). In this he is saying no more than Menéndez Pelayo had said, and saying it less analytically. The latter's *ad hoc* use of the phrase "dramatic poem" recognizes the same fact as Cejador's "pure drama"; a text which may not be potential theater but which makes the same impressions on the mind of the reader.

The most recent and most extensive defense of *La Celestina* as drama has come from the late María Rosa Lida de Malkiel in *La originalidad artística de "la Celestina,"* chapter 1. In fact, all of the more than seven hundred pages of her text are founded on the conviction that the work is dramatic in structure and means of representation, but in that first chapter she examines the contemporary ideas of literary genre, and the development of late medieval and early Renaissance drama. Within the general category of drama she confirms it as an example of "humanistic comedy" (see below, section IV of this chapter), though as a unique and remarkable example of the type. Notably, such older Spanish writers as mention *La Celestina* have seen it as drama also: Lope de Vega, for instance, called it "tragedia famosa."[8] Mrs. Malkiel also presents extensive analysis of the arguments of those who propose a different classification. The time has come to see what these arguments are.

It is certainly significant, as Mrs. Malkiel pointed out, that the refusal to admit *La Celestina* as drama, and the search for an alternative form of classification should occur in the eighteenth century. She cites the English adaptation of 1707, *Celestina or The Spanish Bawd Taken from the Spanish Play of Mateo Alemán*[!] which the adaptors characterize as "unworthy the Name of a Tragedy, Comedy, Tragicomedy, or any thing relating to the Theatre, it having no less than 21 Acts. . . . Indeed his Work is properly Dramatical Dialogues." The first example of the denomination "novel in dialogue" appears to be that which is given by Louis Adrien du Perron de Castera in his *Theatro español* (Paris, 1738).[9] The growth of neoclassical aesthetics with its emphasis on "regularity" and unity of place and time as well as of style, speech, and the social order of the characters made *Celestina* seem an anomaly. Not only does it exceed the prescribed twenty-four hours for the duration of its action and follow that action from place to place, but noble characters perform vulgar deeds, servants and prostitutes are given greater attention than the highborn, and speak with a similar, highly rhetorical mode of speech. Neoclassical literary theory gave attention to drama, epic, and some forms of lyric poetry—the literary forms known to the ancients. The novel, scarcely developed in France beyond imitation of Italian and Spanish originals by the mid-eighteenth century, was left out of account. So, like Limbo, the concept "novel" served as a place to consign those not wholly damned yet not worthy of salvation.

The first figure of authority in Spain to banish *Celestina* from the realm of drama and assign it to that of novel was Leandro Fernández de Moratín, in his *Orígenes del teatro español* (Madrid, 1830). Formed, like his father Nicolás (also a man of letters) in the mold of French aesthetic doctrines, he made the usual objections to the book's acceptance as drama. (As in his mentors, his punctiliousness as to what may be allowed in drama throws into relief the lax unconcern with any accurate definition of "novel" in general, and "dialogue novel" in particular.) His example influenced other critics and editors of the nineteenth century. To this day, *La Celestina* is included in the apparently immortal and certainly interminable library of classics *Biblioteca de autores españoles,* in volume III (1st ed. 1846), entitled *Novelistas anteriores a Cervantes* (Novelists Before Cervantes). I shall not list the writers who, since that time, have used the convenient (because undefined) terms "novel in dialogue," "dramatic novel." Lida (*Originalidad,* pp. 58–78) has done that with abundant documentation and critical pugnacity. It is worth noting, however, that all those who propose such a generic hybrid continue to be particularly attentive to the dramatic characteristics of the work but fail to propose in what way it conforms to the nature of a novel. This easy answer continues to persuade: in his *The Death of Tragedy* (1961), George Steiner referred to *Celestina* as "part novel and part drama."[10]

In 1958, Professor Edwin J. Webber suggested that the various literary works which relate the story of a love, whether in narrative or dramatic form (though not in short poems) should be put together into a separate genre, to be called the "arte de amores."[11] Although medieval concepts of genre seem to us now to have been notoriously loose, no evidence exists that one was ever organized around such a subject matter. Professor Bataillon, however, has seen *La Celestina* as gathering into its field of attraction the literary topics of unhappy love and the whorehouse background to form a new genre—the celestinesque.[12] Such are the problems which Rojas has bequeathed to us. And after the claims that his work is drama, dramatic poem, dialogue novel, novel-drama (i.e., both novel and drama), and finally after the claim that it was its very own genre, it was only to be expected that someone would say it belongs to no genre at all. That, indeed, is Professor Gilman's proposition in *The Art of "La Celestina"* (1956) chapter 7: *"La Celestina* being artistically unique is necessarily without genre. It is 'ageneric,' a monster in the sense that Lope de Vega was a monster." (p. 194). The very quality which, for Menéndez Pelayo, makes it clearly dramatic ("dramatic poem" or "pure drama," in Cejador's words) is for Gilman proof of exemption: "The fundamental condition of this ageneric quality is Rojas' unreserved dedication to dialogue" (p. 194). Also, "I would maintain that it is without genre precisely because it is so profoundly and so uniquely dialogic... It is the necessary product of a creative vision sufficient unto itself and conscientiously in search of its own expression" (p. 195). Yet, for Gilman, the additions of the *Tragicomedia* represent a movement in the direction of the novel: "... the two lovers become increasingly novelistic, increasingly immersed in the inner world of their sentiment, increasingly incapable of a purely dialogic relationship with others" (p. 204). Gilman, more than any other writer on Rojas, has concerned himself with the author's autonomy which, in the process of creation, yields itself to the needs and the vision of the characters. But by writing his own book at the intersection of subjectivities—the characters' (in which Rojas' is presumably immersed) and his own—all of which are equally "real," Gilman makes it impossible for the reader to maintain that aesthetic distance that discussions of form, structure, irony require.[13] His key phrases "dialogic situation" and "meeting of lives" appear to mean little more than the perception of what is common to the structure of all drama: people talking to others, about themselves and others—a world completely realized in dialogue. If there is something more (an existential palpitation), this prevents him from noting ironic asides directed by the author to the reader, by which the work is effectively distanced.[14]

### III *The Idea of Genre*

We are accustomed to fairly recognizable types of literature: lyric, drama, epic, novel, essay, and some subdivisions
(ode, elegy, comedy, tragedy, tragicomedy, and so forth). Such
categories beg some large questions and provoke many more,
and I do not propose to distort such complex questions by sum-
marizing them. It is useful to remember, however, that genre
is not a concept arbitrarily imposed, but it does recognize the
historical reality of literary forms and their distinct functions,
although we often sense the inadequacy of such distinctions.
A sense of genre implies a sense of stylistic and other possibilities without which neither creator nor communication might
be achieved, just as grammatical and syntactic forms are prereq-
uisites for verbal expression, transmission, and reception. Genre
is one way of viewing literary tradition, what has been done
and what, therefore, can be achieved within a particular form.
Novelists write novels because their own expressive needs find
their most adequate form in "the novel." What "the novel" has
become is a showcase of possibilities and resources, and also a
set of formal limits within which the writer's own imagination
can be concentrated.[15] At the same time, each significant work is
new in ways that could not have been predicted from the previous history of the genre, either by recombining familiar
elements or by some more radical innovation. This was stated
in extreme terms by Yury Tyuyanov: "There is no continuing
direct line; there is rather a departure, a pushing away from the
known point—a struggle.... Any literary succession is first of
all a struggle, a destruction of old values and a reconstruction
of old elements."[16]

The generic distinctions with which we are familiar are still
grouped very much as they were by Aristotle in his *Poetics,*
and they have been discussed in the same way by innumerable
comentators from the midsixteenth century on. The most obvious
addition is the novel which did not exist when Aristotle wrote,
but which Renaissance literary theorists saw as the successor to
epic. In the rest—lyric poetry, comedy, tragedy, epic—we can
recognize the principal historical forms of both classical literature and modern literature since the Renaissance. Medieval lit-

erature, however, did not have our familiar distinctions. Aristotle's *Poetics* was known to very few before the sixteenth century, and medieval literature had largely grown afresh from oral kinds (epics, folktales, songs) or from didactic, instructional modes (stories of miracles, lives of saints, chronicles, excerpts from the Bible). The genres, as passed on in manuals of instruction from late Roman to medieval Latin, from Quintilian to Diomedes (late fourth century) become remote from medieval literary tradition in its slow assimilation of new cultures.[17] The Latin texts were easily misunderstood. Genre was confused with style, so comedy could be interpreted as anything written in a "low" style, in contrast to tragedy with its "high" style. Another misunderstanding allowed comedy to apply to any action (not necessarily in dramatic form) which ended happily, and tragedy to any action which ended unhappily. One example of such confusions may be seen in Dante's title of his great poem. His *Divine Comedy* was modeled on epic, but because it ended with joy it was called a comedy. (Needless to say, an allegorical epic in the first person is as far from Greek or Roman experience as a comedy organized into cantos.) The complementary example is found in *The Monk's Tale* by Chaucer:

> Tragedie is to seyn a certeyn storie
> As olde bookes maken us memorie
> Of hym that stood in greet prosperitee,
> And is yfallen out of heigh degree
> Into myserie, and endeth wrecchedly
>                    (*Canterbury Tales*, 1973–1977)

The monk then tells a number of such "tragedies" or stories of misfortune.[18]

## IV  *Medieval Latin Comedy*

In the small store of Latin imaginative literature which survived and continued to be read in medieval schools were the comedies of Plautus and Terence. And not only read but imitated and used as models for student composition in Latin. When twelve lost plays by Plautus were rediscovered in 1429, and the *Commentary* on Terence discovered in 1433, the already popular university authors were given new topical interest. The typical plot of a play by Plautus or Terence would be centered on a young man in love, wondering how to get the girl of his desire. Occasionally it would be more daring, as, for example, in having Jove himself desire the wife of a mortal (*Amphitryon*). Usually, however, the pair are separated by social rank or some other obstacle, such as the girl's father's ambition to make a rich marriage. A quick-witted servant or other accomplice using disguises, pretenses and comic sharp talk moves the events, getting the lovers together, fooling the watchful father or the jealous husband until eventually some lucky stroke brings a happy ending. Thus, love, good fortune, and quick wit—the perennial basic elements in good comedy—define a continuity of motifs from Plautus and Terence to Shakespeare, Lope de Vega, Molière, and Goldoni. Rojas, as we can see, has written a comedy that went wrong. We may note in passing that the term "tragicomedy," invented as a nonsense word by Plautus in the prologue to *Amphitryon*, because it mingled gods and humans, had no precise meaning until a half century after Rojas. His change of title (if indeed it was his) does no more than make obvious to the reader, before he reads, that this is not comedy of the cheerful kind.

Before Rojas, there was a long history of comedy written by medieval authors in Latin, as part of the Latin education in the schools, possibly with public performance in view. By performance, though, medieval students did not mean performance on a stage, because it was believed that the Roman plays were recited rather than acted. We may distinguish two broad phases in the history of these imitations. First, the *elegiac comedies*,[19] (so called because they were generally composed in "elegiac" Latin meters), which originated in the twelfth century. Some of them rehashed scenes from Roman plays, others reworked comic folktales. What they have in common is a concentration on the action, without concern for physical surroundings or motivation or depth of character. Some contemporary characters appear who would not have been available to the Roman comedians—the priests, knights, peasants. But an important change occurs in shifting the burden of the action from the servants to the professional go-between. The servants, instead of abetting, frequently hinder the progress of the love affair, unless they can exploit it for their own profit (e.g., in *Lidia, Geta, Baucis et Traso*). Another important shift within the structure of the play is to give greater importance to the female role. In Roman Comedy, frequently, the girl is there to be got; the intrigue has her as its goal, but the contrivers of the action receive all the audience's attention. In the elegiac comedies, on the contrary, it is not unusual for the situation to be one in which her response is essential: the plot is concerned not solely with outwitting her guardians but with winning her. Thus the go-between develops as a figure skilled in advocacy of the man's claims and in assaulting the woman's reticence. The woman, then, develops as a dramatic figure whose feelings control the outcome. We move from comedy of intrigue toward drama of courtship.

The second broad phase of medieval Latin comedy is represented by *humanistic comedies* (so called because their authors attempted to restore some of the lost classical elements to their work).[20] These plays flourished in the fourteenth, and even more in the fifteenth century. They were longer, subdivided into acts or scenes (the elegiac comedies were short, and individual scenes rudimentary in the extreme). The action might meander among a cast of secondary characters; successive scenes might represent simultaneous actions; the plot would be complicated to the degree that events off-stage would have to be reported. Either verse or prose might be used (Plautus had written in prose). In the course of the fifteenth century it became increasingly common to write comedies in the vernacular but without reducing the flow of plays written in Latin. It is likely that only a small fraction of either kind has survived. Of those that have survived, a number are by men who later achieved renown. They have survived, most likely, because they were the work of brilliant students, which still circulated when the students themselves had departed. And it is because some of these witty and ingenious Latin plays have lived along with the names of their authors that we know that they also were composed at an extraordinarily early age. In their own way they are no less a feat than the composition of *Celestina*.[21]

Of importance in seeing *Celestina* in its own moment of literary history is the fact that these "comedies" increasingly represent a less-than-comic view of love. Though the action generally ends happily, there are desperate episodes, anguished monologues. Also they reflect, along with the theater of Latin antiquity which they imitate on the surface, a range of concerns (honor, reputation, moral standing) which belong clearly to their own time, along with contemporary characters, settings, and references. In particular, one of these plays—*La Venexiana*—written in Italy at about the same time as *La Celestina*, is remarkably similar in its use of dialogue to portray a person and reveal the speaker simultaneously.[22] In fact, many of the particular qualities of *Celestina* can be found in earlier Latin works, which traveled from university to university. A recently edited play, *Poliodorus* (c. 1445?) by Johannes de Vallata, for example, has the go-between, the spiteful servant, and the lesser figures moved by greed. More is known about the dramas written in Italy than about the Spanish ones, and it is clear that the witty, polished *comedie erudite* of Ariosto, Machiavelli, and Bibbiena, in the early sixtenth century, did not spring ready-made from nothing. Their authors had probably served an apprenticeship at the university. Returning to Spain, we may note that the statutes of the University of Salamanca (1538) require the performance of a play by Plautus or Terence every Sunday following Corpus Christi by each college in turn, the winner to receive six ducats. What we do not know—and would very much like to—is by how long this practice preceded the publication of the statutes, and whether original plays were normally written there.

## V  *The Example of the Novel*

Masterpieces are seldom solitary peaks rising sheer from low and featureless ground, and it is becoming clear that, though *La Celestina* may be a masterpiece, it is not a whole genre in itself, as was easy to believe at one time. It is, rather, the preeminent example of a kind of literature, much of which has been lost, but which (like the ancient plays from which it ultimately descends) was formed and sustained in an arena of intense and highly intelligent competition. But the writer

of plays was aware of other literature, too, and the genre which
in some respects shared in Rojas' imaginative world was the so-
called "novel of sentiment" (*novela sentimental*). The misfortunes of Pyramus and Thisbe, and Aeneas Silvius Piccolo-
mini's *Historia de duobus amantibus* (Story of Two Lovers)
circulated widely, as did Boccaccio's *Fiammetta*. But the late
fifteenth century was also a period when novels in Spanish on
the theme of unhappy love were in vogue and were written by
men of talent and sensibility. Diego de San Pedro's *Tractado
de amores de Arnalte y Lucenda* (An Account of the Love of
Arnalte for Lucenda) and *Cárcel de amor* (Love's Prison) published in 1491 and 1492 respectively as well as the works of
Juan de Flores and others develop and make extensive use of
monologue, while also using the highly rhetorical style (rich in
such figures as *dubitatio, exclamatio, pronominatio*) devised for
expressing passionate feelings. Some of the longer speeches of
*La Celestina,* such as Calisto's passionate outburst when he
thinks Melibea has rejected him (act XII)[23] derive more obviously from literature to be read than from models of spoken
speech, though they appear later in stage dramas at moments
of high emotion. (They are not of course confined to Spanish,
as a glance at any Elizabethan play will show.) From these
prose works Rojas may well have learned something of the techniques of emotional display, the rhetorical figures which were
believed to be effective in conveying particular states of mind
and feeling. In particular the solo speech was popular, which,
like the operatic *aria,* permits a passing and unstable moment
of feeling to be projected, expanded, analyzed, and fixed in
verbal form. However, these aspects of *La Celestina* do not alter
the fundamentally dramatic nature of the work; in fact they
endure longer in the history of the drama than they do in that
of the novel, which yields more rapidly to the desire for
current speech, along with accurate representation of the
material world.

The modern temptation to see in Rojas' masterpiece a novel in
dialogue does not, then, arise from the rhetorical aspects of it,
from the stylized emotional climaxes, the monologues, the representation of clashes of feeling in the form of interior debate.
Though these features are highly developed in the fifteenth-

century novel, they were soon discarded by all but the more melodramatic kinds of prose fiction, but they are found everywhere in the European drama of the next two centuries. What is valued as "novelistic" is the rapid dialogue, the creation of the scene through the eyes of the speakers, the apparently unorganized flow of talk, and the absence of any of the conventions of formal unity (three, four, or five acts of regular length, and so on). But here is a paradox. We must agree that these are qualities which made *Celestina* influential in the history of the novel; nevertheless, they are not antidramatic. They simply appear out-of-place when seen against the later development of Renaissance and baroque verse drama with its tight organization all the way from the metrically regular line to the larger unities, formal and thematic, within which the action is developed. They are not out of place when seen against the *previous* history of the drama. The humanistic comedies, both in Latin and in Italian, are written in prose, in an indeterminate number of acts or scenes. The religious dramas of the late medieval period such as the Nativity and Passion plays and the plays on the Old Testament stories, likewise used prose, were spiced with highly topical and colloquial dialogue, and used stage conventions which were much more flexible than those used in the enclosed theaters of Europe in later centuries. The vast "multiple" stages allowed the actors to simulate journeying while they talked, simultaneous action in different places, and to give space a symbolic value which was much reduced in the later commercial theaters.[24] In short, *La Celestina* appears to be an anomaly in part because it has not been seen as the culmination of preceding dramatic traditions. But also, I suggest, there has subsequently been a radical displacement of realistic dialogue from drama to novel, and a reciprocal displacement from novel to drama of externalized, rhetorically organized feeling, of conflicts of sentiment and idea conceived of as *the* action. Only in the sixteenth century do the genres assume the recognizably modern features familiar to us.

## VI  *Drama versus Novel*

It has to be assumed that, irrespective of changing fashions, techniques of representation, and intellectual values, drama and

novel are not ultimately interchangeable, that at some fundamental level of analysis they cannot be confused. We might
begin with the observation of Aristotle (who took it from Plato)
that the verbal arts may be divided according to who speaks:
the poet alone (lyric), the personages alone (drama), or the
poet and the personages alternately (epic).[25] Modifying this,
we could say that in a novel the characters speak and so does
the narrator; there is an "I" who may be one of the characters
telling the story as his own, or he may be situated at any one
of the infinite gradations of distance from the action, all the way
to the anonymous, impersonal voice which says "Once there
was. . . ." As readers, we have to identify ourselves (though
skeptically at times) with the narrative voice if we are to learn
anything at all. In drama we do not identify ourselves with any
speaker or point of view (unless it is propaganda). We are outside looking in, equidistant from all the actors. We do not have
to stand beside any one of them in order to observe the action.
The author likewise is outside, he has excluded himself from
the drama, or, like God, he is everywhere and nowhere at the
same time. He cannot join his characters or speak for them;
if he walks onto the stage, he ceases to be the author and
becomes a character, because drama creates roles, not media
for messages. If he steps forward to address the audience (as in
some political dramas of the 1930s and 1940s) it is a character
called Author who does so, not the Mr. X of real life. Putting
one's ideas, or even one's physical self and one's name, into the
dramatic frame is to turn oneself into something else, into part
of a world which has no reality other than itself. We must bear
this in mind when evaluating Pleberio's final words and asking
whether it is not possible for him to be expressing the truth of
the play as Rojas conceived that truth. Is the play true to Pleberio's vision of the world? or does the play frame and put into
perspective his particular view of the world?

A novel creates, through narrative, a pattern of invented historical events. In it we see more clearly than in life the way
in which a life, or lives, are organized in relation to one another
and to what we call "the environment." These interactions, as
in a true history, are assumed to have finished before we begin
reading; the temporal mode is the past. A drama shows actions

taking place "now." From the point of view of the spectator (or reader) the experiences are not being explained or analyzed (as in a novel) but presented. The substance, as in a novel, is still an image of life in the form of a virtual history[26] but the temporal mode is the present. A future is being created before us and we observe the nexus of desires and interests, ends and means, frustrations and fulfillments in terms of which this future is shaped. The ideas of destiny and fortune are inseparable from the inner workings of drama. The articulation of will, act, and event in a time sequence render the space of the real world largely irrelevant to the space of the stage. The importance of the "blasted heath" or "a distant part of the realm" or "a cottage by the sea" is in what takes place there—its unfurling of what was present in earlier scenes and its discovery of new obstacles or lines of connection with the problematic future that drama struggles with. The importance of space is relative, not absolute;[27] not space as such, but nearness or distance, movement toward or away, rising or falling, entering or leaving, opening or closing.

*La Celestina* deploys a series of actions which lead forward to a catastrophe and which, seen in retrospect, do not cause us to be uneasy. The end, the destiny of the characters, is written into the beginning, into the choices made, into the meta-phorical—and also real—sickness which is installed as the norm of conduct and judgment, into the affront to our (and even Sempronio's) sense of life as a hierarchy of ends and means, of worthy and unworthy objects for men of intelligence and honor. This is particularly obvious in the *Comedia*, where Calisto's fall to his death follows so rapidly upon his seduction of Melibea, and where this "triumph" is achieved so soon after, and at the expense of, the deaths of his accomplices. As was said earlier, the play traces the consequences of a certain way of being in love; death is an adequate symbolization of that train of consequence. The *Tragicomedia*, however, inserts new material between the seduction and Calisto's fall (see below, chapter 7, section III) which alters the economy of the plot. In the opinion of Gilman (*The Art*, pp. 203–6), these changes mark a shift in generic orientation away from the "pure" ageneric art of the *Comedia* to "the very threshold of genre" (p. 206). Since he has committed all his enthusiasm to the genreless quality of *Celestina*, he sees in the new intrigue involving Areusa and Centurio, which is so heavily reminiscent of Plautus, no more than "a hint of theatricality" (p. 204). The extension of the lovers' existence by a month, on the other hand, tends toward novel. "There is, thus, a kind of deceleration, a pastoral languor, a sentimental amplitude, which predicts the novel to come." With the "increased awareness, on the part of the lovers, of the garden around them ... the characters no longer exist just in a situation but even more in a landscape, a private world given meaning by their love" (p. 205); this is confirmation of a "novelistic" trend. But, in truth both drama and novel are capable of containing lyric sections, moments expanded (as we said before) like operatic arias. The idyllic landscape is no more inescapably novelistic than it is foreign to drama, since it is more important as a landscape of the mind, an Eden of the fantasy, than as a real garden. It is not presented as realistic environment, or as the sign of a greater importance being given to the external world, but as a projection of the mind, like Lear's blasted heath, or any of the symbolic landscapes of Shakespearean comedy. Indeed, we have only to look at, and listen to, Calisto and Melibea to observe that they are not more realistically aware of the external world but are ever more engrossed in themselves and each other. More serious for our view of *Celestina* as drama is Gilman's claim that the new material makes Calisto's death more clearly accidental than it was before, clarifying "its absence of fatality" (p. 128). This is not the place to pursue Gilman's argument concerning this new plot and its relation to the meaning of the whole (see below, pp. 157, 161); rather, we will confine our observations to dramatic structure. The death of Calisto is not really "complicated by a new set of circumstances," since those circumstances lead circuitously nowhere and fizzle out in Centurio's damp firecracker. They are a comic deviation and represent *avant la lettre* an Aristotelian *peripeteia*.[28] The chain of causality is no different from what it was in the *Comedia;* it has merely been suspended. Diversions of this nature enrich the dramatic irony, without changing the direction or the level of the plot.

## VII  *Dialogue*

No reader of *La Celestina* has failed to be impressed by the dialogue. With its rhetorical exercises at crucial moments, it does not always match our expectations, but these are matters of historical perspective and serve to remind us that convention is inseparable from language. Speaking the unspeakable emotion is a highly artificial activity, and there is no natural language for it, though we often mistake our more familiar conventions for naturalness. But the dialogue of *Celestina* is the whole medium. Through it the characters communicate with one another, think aloud, debate with themselves (Celestina, act IV; Calisto, acts XII, XIV), expand and open their utterance to buried resentments and hostility (Areusa against Melibea, act IX), slip back and forth between a sharp attention to "now" and a nostalgic evocation of the past.[29] Through it we learn where the action is taking place, for there are no other stage directions. We know where Elicia is when she begins to speak at the beginning of act XV because at the end of the previous act Sosia watched her from his window and commented to Tristán. In act X, while Celestina waits to gain entrance to Melibea's house, Lucrecia tells her "Wait a moment here, by the door" (II, 51). But we also learn *what* is happening through the dialogue, as when Alisa asks her husband why he is tearing his hair (act XXI), or when Melibea begs Calisto not to handle her so roughly (acts XIV, XIX), or when Pármeno, ready to flee in the dark, gleefully describes his posture to Sempronio, thus serving action and psychology in the same words (act XII). The variety of functions of the dialogue is astonishing, and so is the variation of rhythms, from the long ecstatic periods of Calisto's brooding on his love to the brief, nervous exchanges of words, full of suspicions, as Pármeno and Sempronio spar verbally with Celestina before they brutally attack her (act XII).

## CHAPTER 6

# The Characters

## I Some General Questions

THE late María Rosa Lida de Malkiel, in her extensive book on *La Celestina*, noted that the term "character" was losing favor among critics and asked whether it was still possible to discuss Rojas' characters.[1] Generally speaking, it is a fact that certain old-fashioned views of characters in literature are no longer heard. We no longer look upon them as old friends, or try to imagine them talking about subjects in which they never expressed any interest. We don't try to build a life off-stage for Lady Macbeth or Ophelia. But if these sometimes amusing and generally harmless games have less appeal than they once did, the assumptions on which they were based have not been destroyed. We expect that a fictional person will have a certain temperament and moral qualities, and that these characteristics will be expressed in what he or she says and does (i.e., through dialogue and action). More important than the chronicling of every thought or instinctive movement or personal foible of taste and judgment, is consistency; our feeling that the character is grounded adequately in its situation and responds acceptably to the claims the author makes of it. "Consistency" does not mean that the character has to be at all times predictable, for such a character could not hold our interest for long. It does mean that even if we are surprised by a character's act or thought, the feeling of surprise must not be accompanied by incredulity but rather must give new insight, or add a new dimension. It is not easy to say when the elements in a complex character have gotten out of hand and consistency is destroyed. A stable character may change under stress, without sacrificing credibility. A sympathetic character may commit an enormity, as Othello does in murdering Desdemona, and still we do not cease to accept

104

him. As we read a novel or watch a play we carry with us our experience of real people and, in particular, of their variability, their capacity for self-contradiction, their tendency to combine a faultless grasp of reality on one level of their being with the most regrettable blindness on another level.

In a novel or a play (and often in life), a character is perceived only as a factor in a situation or in a process in time. Thus, not all characters are equally important or equally developed. Moreover, there are many kinds of novels and plays, so that the proportions which may be observed between character and action are infinitely variable. A medieval play on the birth of Christ, or on his trial and execution, leaves little room for character as such. The events and their universal significance are what matter. Characterization may be developed to a small degree in such figures as the shepherds or the Magi, or among the gossips of Nazareth, but here the purpose is in the function once more: to ground a supernatural event in the concrete world of particular people at a particular time. The principal personages cannot be discussed as characters at all. At another extreme we find Samuel Beckett's *Molloy*, an uninterrupted monologue—uninterrupted, that is, except when the speaker chooses to interrupt himself—about himself and his sense of the meaning of his experiences as he recalls them. Here the speaker is really two people, the talking self and the talked-about self, subject and object, the perceiver and the perceived. If we were to use the word "characterization" in such a case, we would have to give it a rather special meaning, because there is no situation external to the character. The situation, in fact, is internal to the character (or rather the two characters: self as speaker, self as object of recollection and reflection). The situation is not the room in which Molloy has found himself but the mental space, the eddies of memory, the perspective of frozen time, along which the words are disposed.

From these examples we can see that neither a narrative which sets out events having mythic status, an objectifying and universalizing function (the life of Christ, or the return of Orpheus from Hades), nor experiences which are wholly internalized by a single speaker can allow us to use the word "character" as it is commonly understood. But they do throw into prominence the fact that "character," however understood, and however residual the concept may become in given examples, exists only in the function of a whole, a total structure involving the situation, the nature of the events, the fabric of imagined time and space. The consistency of a character is only one within a web of many consistencies or articulations of proportion within the work. Our understanding of character in literature depends not only on our experience of people, but on our recognition that plays and novels are composed of a complex interrelation of parts.

Our extreme examples (others imposing different kinds of constraint on the concept of character could easily be found) are not irrelevant to our analysis of *La Celestina*. Rather, they are analogous to two ways in which influential critics have read the play. Marcel Bataillon, the most eminent proponent of the "exemplary" reading of *La Celestina* presents it as primarily didactic.[2] His commentary reveals a moral intent in every aspect of the book. Consequently the pattern of events is what carries the message, and the catastrophe traces the passions, the follies, the egoism, etc. of the characters to a proper and just conclusion. What we have said about a play or other embodiment of mythical plot—that in universalizing the events it severely limits the possibility of individual characters—is then applicable to the work of critics who look at plays or novels in terms of moral or other nonliterary categories. Bataillon's interpretation tends toward the presentation of the persons as *types* (selfish lover, wicked bawd, disloyal servant, and so on). On the other hand, Stephen Gilman would like to discard the notion of character in favor of a more existential terminology.[3] There is continual dialogue, without any objective third person to fix and give continuity to our perceptions of the speakers. So, he says, there is little use in abstracting a "Celestina" or "Calisto" from the dialogue in which they live (p. 57). Thus, we find Gilman writing about "Rojas' art of creating human lives in the first and second person" (p. 58). He views the play as a series of encounters by discrete subjectivities in "dialogic situations" and, by stressing what Martin Buber has made familiar as the I-Thou relationship, makes each person the center of his or her own drama. Each of these dramas involves the *tú* ("thou," person addressed) and the speaker's own awareness of self, of past actions, past existence, nostalgia, image in the eyes of the other, and so on. Thus we move toward a reading of *La Celestina* as a series of monologues, inner dramas tangentially related to one another. In fact, there are many occasions when the "lives" of which Gilman speaks are characters under a new name, construed from the text by the accustomed means.[4] Ironically, the repeated use of the term "life" takes us back again to a mode of criticism which threatens to cut the character adrift from his role in the work, and from the author.[5]

Even with their very diverse procedures, both Bataillon and Gilman recognize that characters are defined by their function in a text. We must also observe that no work of literature can be wholly independent of its predecessors. If it were independent, it would be incomprehensible. This is another way of saying that literary works are (from one point of view) dependent on convention and tradition, like language itself. As in the history of a language, minute deviations from precedent can acquire an unsuspected capacity for meaning. So verbal art creates its own conditions out of both continuity and change.

## II *Calisto*

One of the ways in which an author may creatively exploit a convention in his literary tradition is by revaluing its "motifs" or constituent narrative elements.[6] A well-born young man, handsome and voluble, might well serve as hero for a romance of love. The reader coming to *Celestina* on its first appearance could have been familiar with the Latin plays of Plautus and Terence which were widely read and imitated in university circles in the fifteenth century, and with a wave of sentimental novels by such writers as Juan de Flores, Diego de San Pedro, Pedro Manuel Jiménez de Urrea, Juan Rodríguez del Padrón, to mention only the best known of the native authors.[7] In general, the plays found a happy ending, though the obstacles might appear formidable, whereas the novels stressed the unhappy and often the tragic, side of love. With *La Celestina*, a reader might have hesitated to formulate his expectations. Unlike his counterparts in drama, who usually find a quick-witted servant or other schemer close at hand to help him get his girl, Calisto is accompanied by no such sharp fellow. Also, whereas the heroes of the dramatic pieces might work actively and cheerfully on another front (in disguise for example), Calisto plunges into despair and hides in the darkness of his room. Then again, the exalted language which he uses to address Melibea, seeing divine perfection in her, or his declaration that he is not a Christian but a "Melibean," reflects a tradition of passionate lyric poetry (which also flows into the sentimental novel in fifteenth-century Spain) weighted with images of suffering and death (see below, chapter 7). Thus the reader cannot tell from his first impression of the action and its tone what kind of character Calisto is or what kind of outcome to expect. He must not draw conclusions from antecedent literature but must read attentively.

Calisto's social status is fairly clearly defined by his pastime of falconry, which was an aristocratic exercise; by the various references of Melibea to his nobility (II, 86 and 196, among others); and by the *argumento* which precedes the action. He clearly belongs to a prestigious family; in act XIV he recalls that the judge who sentenced Sempronio and Pármeno ate his father's bread (II, 124), and therefore owed him better service. What kind of dependency these words denote is not made clear (Calisto's father could have been an old-fashioned feudal landlord or a city merchant who had paid for the judge to go to university in his youth). However, they do reveal a certain confusion in Calisto's mind between justice and self-interest, between honor interpreted as avoidance of scandal and honor understood as integrity. Just as literary precedent is of little help in enabling us to determine initially what manner of person Calisto is, and what his destiny is to be, so we are given only enough information about his social rank to know vaguely that he is well-to-do and influential, but not enough to know his standing in the town, what his household is like, etc. Again, Rojas forces us to watch events, listen to words, and make our own judgment of persons from seeing how they conduct themselves in their relationships, rather than from their social roles.

It is a notable fact, however, that we never encounter, nor

even hear of, any members of Calisto's household other than
the servants who participate in the action. No mother or father
ever sends to know why he is not at table for dinner, or to
inquire about his irregular hours. He is completely alone, with
his two valets. He moves only between his house and Melibea's,
with one visit to church, for variation. Fleeting mentions of
friends, relatives, are mere words, never attached to any concrete presence that we can feel in the spaces of his life not
occupied by Melibea.[8] Who besides Calisto occupies the house;
whom he knows in the town; how he has spent his life; what
is his family's role in the community—these and many other
similar questions have to remain unanswered. To judge from
the action of the play, he might be an orphan; yet we would
have no positive justification for claiming that he is, only the
absence of certain information that we are accustomed to being
given. It may well be that he represents the idle rich who value
leisure and display, in contrast to the old aristocracy with its
ethic of service and responsibility, as J. A. Maravall has argued.[9]
But on the other hand, the absence of activity in Calisto's house,
and the isolation of his life from friends, youthful companions
(whom did he go hawking with?), the lack of any family or
social nexus, cannot be explained solely in realistic terms. On the
contrary, it is precisely the failure of the book to provide
answers to questions like these which should make us cautious
of trying to read it as a wholly realistic work.

For María Rosa Lida de Malkiel, Calisto's basic trait of character is his selfishness,[10] and almost everything about him can be
seen as an aspect of this quality. His isolation is indicative of
his "pure individualism, his asocial quality."[11] Other persons,
his servants for example, are made use of as instruments; at the
time when they and Celestina die, Calisto no longer needs them,
so he self-righteously moralizes over their deaths.[12] These
observations are exact; yet they are not wholly satisfactory to
the extent that they imply, once again, a basically realistic conception of the structure of a character. In the same chapter,
the late Mrs. Malkiel also observed his lack of adjustment to
reality and his swings from excitement to depression, which
she diagnoses as symptoms of a retarded adolescence.[13] While
accepting the truth of the observations on Calisto's behavior

and the validity of assigning such acts to a typical personality (young, egotistical, self-absorbed, etc.), we must be careful to distinguish between realism and verisimilitude. Mrs. Malkiel argued for a realism of conception which we believe to be more appropriate to nineteenth-century novels in which the given elements of character, working upon a given set of social circumstances, produce a certain set of consequences. I believe this to be mistaken as a way to approach *La Celestina* and would prefer to say that acts and motives provide a pattern of *events*, while recognizing nevertheless that Rojas has taken care to provide such fixed traits as will give coherence and consistency to the actors. This distinction is more than a matter of words; it is the question of artistic ends and means.

Unlike most stories and plays about being in love (*Romeo and Juliet*, Chaucer's *Troilus and Criseyde*, for example) we never see the protagonist, Calisto, when he is out of love. This, in itself, should be sufficient warning against trying to reconstruct a complete character for Calisto. His first words are those addressed to Melibea, whose irritable reception then drives him to melancholy reclusion and to all the consequences that we have seen. Like a poem, a love-lyric, the form of *La Celestina* is coextensive with a state of mind. For there to be realism of character, we would have to be shown the other Calisto, the one *before* his fall into love. But Rojas has clearly not done that, and he just as clearly has shown the progress of a passion, a way of being in love, with its results for the protagonist and the other persons in the cast. It is important that we recognize this fact and seize its significance. What we witness in the first words of the play is the birth of a passion which transforms the subject. The action of *La Celestina*, seen from the perspective of Calisto, is his existence in love, the reorientation and subordination of his life to this passion. From the moment when the action begins, no other reality exists for Calisto. The form of the play mirrors the mind of Calisto: nothing from outside his situation of passion can exist within it. There are no social relationships that do not serve his passion. Mentions of the parents, friends, the "they" who occupy Calisto's house resemble so many vague and distant echoes from another reality, which indeed they are. They belong to the world of Calisto as it was before his fall into love, before the abrupt beginning of the dialogue in act I marked a rupture with the normal familial and social web.

When Dante fell in love with Beatrice, it was as if he had begun a new life. The feeling is not unique, for many persons have had the experience of entering a new existence, of having their lives made fresh and radiant, given new meaning, by love. Shortly after the death of Beatrice, Dante marked this phase in his life by collecting together the sonnets he wrote to celebrate her, linking them with commentaries in prose, and calling this poetic autobiography *La Vita Nuova* (The New Life, c. 1292). It is a chronicle of feelings, and it attributes to his love for Beatrice his rebirth in a new self, more tender, more caring, more noble in feeling, more patient, more generous, and more sociable than the old. Beatrice is the light of his mind and symbol of all beauty; to love her is to know goodness and harmony. So by his love an order, an exquisite poise is established, in his feelings; passion is quelled, a taut serenity achieved; and the mind is enthroned above the senses. If we compare this with the experience of Calisto, we see that the latter's "new life" is the very opposite of Dante's. From the moment that he speaks to Melibea, he seeks the dark, avoids company, is absorbed in himself, and cares only for the gratification of his passion and his sensuality—the oppositions can be completed without difficulty. Where Beatrice opened a new reality to Dante, Calisto loses all sense of reality; where Dante is elevated to divine beauty and wisdom, Calisto is debased to blasphemy and to receiving help from a devotee of Satan. I do not mean to suggest that Rojas literally took the moral and conceptual pattern of Dante's *La Vita Nuova* and turned it upside down. Dante's work was known, of course, but its ideal of the ennobling love which disciplines the soul had entered the poetic tradition. It is that tradition (refined by generations of troubadours, and of which Dante furnishes the richest example), a tradition which embodies a search for the highest expression of love between man and woman, an adventure worthy of the best minds, which Calisto so wretchedly betrays.

Calisto's solitariness, his lack of contact with others, then, is less a matter of individualism in his personality than that of a symbolic reversal of what love should achieve. And the same may be said of the other aspects of his behavior. He is unable to separate dream and reality (acts XIII, XIV) or sacred and profane people and things (he laments briefly for the deaths of Pármeno, Sempronio, and Celestina, but they have become unnecessary as tools anyway—act XIII). He sleeps while others toil for him. He insults the faithful servant Pármeno and rewards the ingratiating Sempronio. Reckless rather than generous in his gifts and promises to Celestina, we have seen that he is also venal in his indignation against the judge (act XIV). He trusts Pármeno only after the latter has been corrupted, and then he allows himself to be duped by both servants, believing that rogues are loyal, cowards valiant. He is impatient for the hours to fly so that he may be with Melibea: then, when he is in her arms, he prays that the dawn may never come (in the *Comedia* he does not live to see the dawn). If we were to identify a basic quality in Calisto, rather than the selfishness indicated by Mrs. Malkiel, it would have to be a negative one, and intellectual as well as moral: an absence of judgment. "Love makes the foolish man wise": Ovid and Juan Ruiz said it for a laugh,[14] but many medieval poets claimed to be better men for the effects of love. Not Calisto, though: he is crazed by love and misses the mark in all his judgments. He shows himself hasty in speech to Melibea, hasty in rushing to hide in the dark, hasty in wanting to batter down Melibea's door at their first interview (act XII), though it could only ruin them both; and hasty in wanting to rip her beautiful clothes off in the garden (acts XIV, XIX). (Where is that courtesy which love is supposed to breed in the lover?) With the same impetuousness and lack of judgment he rushes to the help of Sosia and Tristán (act XIX), believing that they are incapable of looking after themselves, and just as impetuously he reverses his misplaced trust in Pármeno and Sempronio.

The failure of courtesy which we noted in Melibea's garden is also a failure of judgment of a certain kind—decorum, a sense of what is due to the person or required by the occasion. Often a failure of decorum may be nothing more than ignorance or uncertainty about what convention requires, but Calisto's failure is more serious, as we see repeatedly, for example, when he uses the language of religious devotion in speaking to and about Melibea; when he uses the same language in addressing Celestina as he would in addressing his love; or when he embraces and fondles Melibea's belt, to the disgust of Celestina and the servants (act VI). Calisto is unhinged. His kind of love is the antithesis of that which harmonizes the faculties and brings the lover to an understanding of a new dignity and beauty. His passion, far from endowing him with any higher understanding, has deprived him of the most common understanding. Reversing day and night, unaware of either time or necessity, he is removed from the world's natural pulse and rhythm. He can respond to nothing but the flux of feeling and the allurements of fantasy.

### III  *Melibea*

Readers of Spain's seventeenth-century drama and novels are familiar with the young woman who, on receiving a declaration of love, responds with indignation and asks, rhetorically, what lapse in her demeanor can have given encouragement to such boldness. "I am a virtuous woman, a woman of honor, and not to be trifled with" is the substance of all such speeches. Melibea's repulse of Calisto is of this kind. And, like her counterparts in the later comedies, she responds most vehemently to the man she is destined to love. The comedies of the seventeenth century usually end in marriage, but the encounter and the defensive reflex are the same. A society in which women were closely guarded, chaperoned, and given their prescribed place by men, allowed them no occasion for public expression of feeling. Marriages were mostly arranged by parents, especially when the undivided inheritance of an estate or the acquisition of some new property was at stake. It is perhaps only a slight exaggeration to say that being a woman in a Mediterranean society is like being a converso in a community of old Christians; every word, every gesture, every glance must conform to a standard of proper behavior if the woman is not to be thought "shameless," to invite the wrath of the men of the family, and, perhaps, to become an outcast.[15] In such circumstances we cannot exaggerate the shock—of fear, anxiety, possibly accompanied by secret pleasure—on first being addressed by a young man, suddenly, alone, and in terms like those used by Calisto. In the social constraints which hedge her around we may see a continuation of old poetic motifs such as the girl's strict guardians (the Latin *custos*, the Provençal *gardador*). In her complaint that a girl may not take the initiative in love, we sense the presence of late medieval debate on the freedom of women to choose their mates.

It has been suggested that Melibea's fury is caused by Calisto's *manner* of approaching her.[16] The argument goes that conduct in such situations was governed by the rules of "courtly love," as set out in the treatise of Andreas Capellanus and elsewhere, and that Calisto used the wrong formula, one which presumed too great a familiarity. Melibea was then justly angered by his clumsiness and lack of tact. I will not give all the reasons why I find this explanation unacceptable; some have to do with the nature of Andreas' treatise; more obviously, it is not supported by anything which Melibea later says or does, and Calisto has yet more clumsiness to offer in later scenes (in act XIX she calls him a "model of courtesy" and complains of his rough handling, all in the same breath). Finally, the hypothesis is unnecessary. Melibea is not angered by Calisto's manner but fearful of being addressed by a man at all. Her response is due to fear, anxiety, and overly defensive self-protection, as we note later, in act X, where Celestina skillfully eases Melibea's restraints and brings an unacknowledged love to the threshold of her startled and trembling gaze (see our commentary on act X in chapter 4).

This reading of Melibea is supported by her sensitivity to much that is outside herself—in contrast to Calisto. To put it differently; her preoccupation with her offense against God, honor, reputation, her father's good name, her position as heiress, which emerges later, all of this internalized and compressed, gave force to her repulse of Calisto in act I. By a brilliant use of irony, it is her irremediable love which makes her conscious of these values in herself only at the moment when she is betraying them. As María Rosa Lida de Malkiel noted, she is aware of being part of a family and a society, and this awareness participates in her judgment of her acts. Unlike Calisto, she does not suppress her sense of shame but sincerely regrets that for her love she must quietly betray trust. This is to say that she does not use words like "honor" in a self-serving way, as Calisto does. She is fascinating because Rojas achieves in her, and in no other character, such expansion and deepening of self-awareness, increasing in painful clarity as her end approaches. For this reason, she is the one figure that might be called tragic.

The seduction of Melibea's will by Celestina does not represent a reversal of her personality, as I hope to have demonstrated, but an unloosing of personal energies. One might be tempted to speak of "freedom" or "liberation," but these words are too tarnished by their use as slogans. For the energies which are released in Melibea are not those of individual creativity and fulfillment but those of the species; the sensual drives, the instinct for survival, the pleasure of power. Let us briefly consider the last of these, the pleasure of power. However much she may regret deceiving her parents, she quickly masters the art. Even in her earlier dealings with Celestina, she engineers the old woman's return by promising the prayer to Saint Apollonia—but not now: Celestina must come back secretly for it (act IV). She derives intimate satisfaction from teasing Calisto (act XII), making as if to reject him so as to hear his declaration. Unlike Calisto, she does not consult her servant, she gives orders; and in the last moments of her life she gives clear and ruthless commands to her father, which maintain a clear line of connection with her irascibility of act I. We saw (in the commentary on act XX) that Melibea speaks directly to her father for the first time in that act, when her alienation from him is greatest and is symbolized by the physical distance which she puts between herself and him. It is then that she reaches the height (literally and metaphorically) of willfulness, commanding her father to be silent and denying him the right to show his love and mercy or to kill the fatted calf for her. Finally, she wills her own destruction and damnation. With the same absoluteness that she showed in rejecting marriage, she now rejects life without Calisto. Earlier in that same night the expanded *Tragicomedia* leaves no doubt of her tenderness toward Calisto, of which he shows himself characteristically unworthy. A tenderness which transcends their literary fantasies of love, and reaches in vain for repose. In all these various ways, she could scarcely present a clearer image of the human condition.

## IV  *Celestina*

Antecedents for Celestina may be found in Roman comedies, in Ovid's *Ars amatoria,* where lovers are advised to seek the help of an experienced practitioner, and in the same writer's *Amores,* where old Dipsas is devoted to exploiting the young men who need her services. The type is developed further in the medieval Latin comedies (verse dialogues not meant for acting) which circulated in the twelfth and thirteenth centuries, the best known of which is *Pamphilus.*[17] This dialogue has in its cast an Old Woman who is far closer to Celestina than the preceding examples, since she is given a major role in the action, which is to induce Galatea to accept Pamphilus as lover, and her powers of persuasion have therefore to be seen in operation, not merely advertised. The development, however, is uneven, and she is still far from the complexity of Celestina in the range of her character. The intellectual and moral implications of the go-between are greatly developed in the Duenna of the *Romance of the Rose.* In Spanish, the closest precedent is Trotaconventos in the *Libro de buen amor* (Book of Good Love) by Juan Ruiz, Archpriest of Hita (two versions: 1330 and 1343).[18] She has great personal energy and industry, pride in herself and her profession, and an epicurean philosophy to sustain it. But she, like her predecessors in Latin, is seen in relation to two persons only: the man who has commissioned her and the girl she is soliciting. Her dealings with the various women in the *Book of Good Love* do not vary greatly in verbal approach or psychological subtlety, and she relies heavily on persuasion through stories to counter the women's defensive use of fables and other cautionary tales. Only Rojas frees his bawd from such formal restraints, enlarges upon her diversity of professional operations, and makes explicit her trust in witchcraft. Finally, and most important, only Rojas gives to Celestina a place at the center of the work, where she affects the lives of all the rest of the cast and creates a network of interests which converge upon her; makes her, in short, the vortex into which they are all drawn. Her influence continues after her death in act XII.[19]

Celestina: the significance of her name is part of the rich

tissue of ironies in the book. As a retired prostitute herself and
now keeper of a whorehouse, dabbler in magic and witchcraft,
maker of potions and cosmetics, and restorer of broken maidenheads she has more obvious affinities with her accomplice, the
Devil, who also is a master of false appearances. There is
nothing celestial about Celestina, but her name is appropriate,
and not only because it indicates the opposite of her real nature.
There is also nothing truly divine about Melibea or Calisto's
desire for her, but he calls her a goddess and makes a heaven
of his desire. Celestinas exist because men create paradises of
the fantasy and require the fantasy to be made flesh. In such
artificial paradises Celestina is indeed a celestial broker, inter-
ceding for the suppliant with the powers of darkness. If the
reader were to imagine a negative travesty of the Virgin Mary,
he could not find a more suitable model, in all particulars, than
Celestina.

Calisto desires Melibea. Sempronio, who has brought Celestina in to realize Calisto's desires, looks for his reward, but his
desire comes into conflict with hers; they both want money and
valuables. Celestina, unable any longer to enjoy the pleasures
of the flesh, except wine, is set upon accumulatiing the one
thing into which all others can be converted. Money, of course,
is the instrument of all professional activities, so her desire for
it is a condition of her professionalism. (That is why prostitution is the oldest profession; every other profession must have
begun by not being a profession. The prostitute, like the paid
soldier, must always be an alien in a feudal or tribal structure
based on loyalty and personal service.) Her need to make
Calisto's servants her accomplices means that she has two greedy
men with the same appetite, and money (unlike sex) becomes
less as it is shared around. Thus, tension and suspicion grow
between Celestina, Sempronio, and Pármeno until, partly in
reaction against their own cowardice earlier that night, the
two men kill the old woman (see commentary on act XII). A
medieval mind would have seen the connection between the
two phases of Celestina's career—whore and procuress—without difficulty: they are the same desire, *cupiditas* or greed, but
directed to different objects.[20] Not all of her desire is redirected
to money, however. As she says after putting Pármeno into bed

with Areusa and watching them begin, she still has the taste of it in her empty gums (act VII). She would not be the "celestial" figure that she is if she did not overflow with love![21]

Celestina is the most energetic of all the persons in the play. She is always moving, planning, watching, and ensuring that Elicia or Areusa make the most of their opportunities. Nothing, apparently, is left to chance. She is a "great provider" for the girls who share her establishment, as well as for her old age. She has been as industrious in her life as Pleberio, her contemporary, in his. But while he has ascended on Fortune's wheel and can look out with pride on the estate which he intends to pass on to Melibea, she has to look back (and frequently does) in order to recall the prosperity she once had, the beauty that turned the noblest heads in town. (This is but one example of a complementariness in Celestina and Pleberio not noticed by critics.) With her vigor, then, goes a debilitating nostalgia for past triumphs. She can see in herself living evidence for the mutability of Fortune, which gives her a kind of moral authority over Elicia and Areusa, as she urges them to enjoy the hour and make hay while the sun shines and laments the aches and unremittting toil of old age (especially in act IX). Calisto is engrossed in his fantasies of the delights of Melibea's garden; Celestina risks losing *her* footing on reality as her mind leaps into the past at the sight of Melibea's fresh complexion, Areusa's naked body, Pármeno's boyish vigor, a table laden with food, and so on. The rhetoric of her trade ("enjoy youth") is becoming dangerously confused, on the one hand, with the divagations of memory in search of her own lost paradise, and on the other, with the urge to grasp what profit she can.

Before the disaster occurs, however, we see two notable successes, and they are achieved through the medium of her greatest resource: her tactical use of language. She is a continual talker, as her profession, or various professions, require, but talk is a flexible instrument at the service of shrewd insight and calculation of motives and weaknesses. She is able to adjust the tone and level of her speech to the person she is addressing, to excite curiosity by delays and circumlocutions, to feign humility and care, or to be silent and wait for an opening. In her seductions of Pármeno and Melibea we see the most brilliant displays of her verbal craft. In the first case she assumes the role of substitute mother to the orphan Pármeno, a transference which is made easier for her because the real mother was a professional colleague of hers (for whom she now expresses admiration) and thus she knew him as a small child. Also, she tempts him away from his stern loyalty to Calisto, through his adolescent sensuality (see commentary on act VII). Like a mother, she envelops him with care and soft words, gently rebukes him for not respecting her judgment, and finally rewards him for good behavior. She has succeeded in destroying him by confusion, by substituting her own self and role for his image of the good. We see confirmed what was evident in her relations with Calisto—she is the negative image or counterpart of bountiful providence, fulfillment, and joy.

Her seduction of Melibea is different. The girl refuses to hear Calisto's name; yet she feels an unbearable pain that she does not know the cause of. The name of Calisto and the name of the disease must be brought together by physician Celestina in order to achieve a cure. For Melibea, as for Calisto and Pármeno, she is Mother (*madre*); once again she spuriously replaces the familially and socially mediated values that have given structure to a personality. We cannot adequately detail the verbal means by which this is achieved, but they include subtly improvising the role of physician which Melibea's "sickness" requires; listening, gently probing, soothing the harsh facts with warm generalities; inviting absolute frankness and confidence, thus transferring the patient's will from its customary moral supports to the desire for cure, until finally she is ready; and then, like a good herbalist, inserting the new poison that will drive out the old. All of this is done with variations of pace and tempo to correspond with Melibea's fear and uncertainty or flashes of defensive irascibility. Finally, like the Devil whom she patronizes, she despises her clients. Her appearances contain many asides in which she mutters contemptuously against Calisto, Melibea, and Pármeno.

## V  *Calisto's Servants*

As María Rosa Lida de Malkiel pointed out, a fundamental structural frame for the characters is what she called *geminación,* or doubling.[22] Characters form pairs, either because that is a necessary aspect of their role (as with parents or lovers) or because the author has chosen these pairings as a means of developing important parallels and contrasts and of enriching the contexture of the action. Such pairings need not remain fixed and are not confined to characters but can be seen in events, for example, in Celestina's two triumphs (over Pármeno and Melibea), the two garden scenes (acts XIV, XIX), and other smaller motifs. Sempronio and Pármeno begin as opposites in temperament and in the manner of conceiving their duty to Calisto, but they are identical in destiny. That destiny is shaped by Celestina, but its necessity or final cause is in Calisto.

Sempronio is the first person to hear Calisto talk about his love for Melibea. He replies sardonically, affects superiority, and chewing on old maxims about the inferiority of women: they are not worth the trouble. His own farcical upstairs-downstairs dialogue with Elicia (I, 61–63) would seem to confirm this, did he but realize it. He is the older, more respected of the two servants, a man who has long since decided on which side his bread is buttered, that a servant's job is to please the master, not to have convictions. With his young master, he has an opportunity to impress as well, to display his vulgarity and call it experience. Rojas (or whoever wrote act I) has broken with the tradition of Latin comedy in the character of Sempronio. He is the one who has the idea of calling in Celestina, but he is not in the line of descent of such figures as Plautus' Pseudolus, because he does not identify himself completely with his master's interest, as the Roman comic servants do, and he himself is not a constructive schemer. His only concern is to profit from the affair, and to this end he encourages Calisto to be generous in his rewards to Celestina, expecting that she will go shares with him. In this he has misjudged her. This single thread of self-interest, decorated with the rather shoddy trappings of self-importance (a taste for proverbs, instructive examples, and the like) is present from the first when he debates with himself whether to go into Calisto's room or not (I, 37–39). If he does not, Calisto may kill himself with despair; if he does, Calisto may turn violent against him. Characteristically, the next stage of the dilemma is to decide whether or not it would be to his advantage if Calisto killed himself; whether he might stand accused or whether, perhaps, there might be a little legacy for him. The play has hardly begun when we find ourselves listening to the dialectics of egoism, which will continue throughout the core of the action.

Pármeno begins as the antithesis of Sempronio: young, bright, alert, his beard is just beginning to sprout, and he is physically self-conscious. He is also at the age of uncomplicated moral outrage and has not been shaped into servility. Sempronio and Celestina both find him a nuisance: by winning him over, she can prevent him from warning Calisto to look to his good name, and at the same time, she can make him more companionable to Sempronio. This alliance, forged by Celestina, will be the instrument of her own death, because she has unloosed a greed which is in direct competition with her own. Between Celestina's subversive conversation with Pármeno and the complete submission which he shows as he and Sempronio wait for their master outside Melibea's house, there are some momentary reversals. But the final thrust against his integrity is given by Calisto who shows himself unworthy of loyalty (Acts II, VI). Since he is unsentimental, Pármeno does not idealize anyone— Calisto, Areusa, or Celestina. Before Celestina corrupted his mind, he could distinguish people from his own duty toward them. The unworthiness of Calisto did not prevent his loyally speaking up, and the mother-image in Celestina did not intimidate him. After his conversion he is an unworthy servant, but even then he does not idealize the mother in Celestina, as she discovers at her death.

After Sempronio and Pármeno have died, they are replaced by Tristán and Sosia who are promoted. Sosia is a stable-lad with mud on his boots, boyish and awkward, with some vanity and a lot of sense. Tristán is more experienced and wiser. Again, a contrasting pair, an older and a younger partner, one ready to advise and another willing to learn. That is how the world works, when it does work. More important than the contrast of complementary traits between Tristán and Sosia, is that between this pair of servants and the former pair. Pármeno, after he lost his innocence and his self-respect, gloried in his readiness to run away when he and Sempronio were on duty as bodyguards to Calisto, and he went wild with joy on inventing some good reason for not exposing himself to risk. *Corruptio optimi pessima.* Tristán and Sosia, who have, presumably, seen less service and have not until now been personal valets, are sober and reliable. They have no difficulty in standing firm when the rowdy but cowardly Centurio sends a friend in his place to attack Calisto.

Sosia does momentarily have his head turned by Areusa, who says she is in love with him so as to wheedle information about Calisto's visits to Melibea. But Tristán sobers him with matter-of-fact questions which prick the bubble of his vanity. Isn't Areusa beautiful and elegant and isn't she solicited by lots of rich handsome men and couldn't she have any one she wants, so would she really love you with your muddy boots and smell of horses? Tristán is firm and tactful; Sosia sees himself in the mirror, recognizes the justice of Tristán's remarks, and is properly contrite. These are the first honest voices that we have heard in a long time, having nothing to conceal, not on the make, not deluded, not driven by fantasies. In this sense they are to be contrasted with everyone (except the earlier Pármeno) and not just with their predecessors. They belong to a world without Celestina and without artificial paradises. They witnessed the execution of Pármeno and Sempronio; they also carry away the body of "our dear master" (II, 185).

## VI  *Lucrecia*

Lucrecia is the faithful servant of Melibea, who laments the lapses of her mistress, makes sharp asides, but always protects her from discovery. Comically anxious and prim at one moment, at another she is suddenly aware of being isolated and of not getting any of what others are enjoying. As Calisto and Melibea embrace in the garden and she keeps watch, with her teeth on edge, she nevertheless curses the servants who are outside and have not noticed her. This recalls the banquet (act XIX) when Areusa, knowing that Lucrecia is listening at the door, celebrates the freedom of their way of life and deplores the miseries of those who are in service. Lucrecia does very little, but such is the richness of the play that her way of being—meek, proper and dutiful but, tormented by the sight and sounds of lovers, also a *voyeuse*—falls beautifully into place.

## VII   *Elicia and Areusa*

These two prostitutes (and cousins) are the visible part of the network which Celestina has spread through the city (act III; I, 133) drawing girls into her trade. They are not associated with her in the same degree, however. Elicia, as we see in act I, is part of Celestina's establishment, and has been trained in the profession, though certain aspects of it repel her, and she refuses to learn them (act VII). (Celestina's establishment is in decline: girls do not work as they used to in the great days of her prime!) Areusa is an independent girl of pleasure, who lives apart, but who can be counted upon to repay favors, for example, by breaking in young Pármeno. They react differently to the deaths of Celestina and the servants. Elicia goes into mourning and public weeping; she had seen the deed herself. She refuses to join with Areusa but sits at home with her grief. Areusa's reaction when she hears the news from Elicia is vehement and angry. Whereas Elicia is submissive to misfortune, Areusa plans revenge on Melibea (who, in her reasoning, is to blame) by having her lover waylay Calisto by night. Here is a resurgence of that bitter jealousy against Melibea, compounded of personal envy and social resentment, that almost wrecked the banquet in act IX.

## VIII   *Alisa and Pleberio*

Melibea's parents have two principal functions. First, they represent authority. They are consequently the focal point of the feelings of shame which Melibea feels after she has yielded to Celestina's persuasion. For Calisto also, her father is a formidable presence though they never meet. He imagines Pleberio as a man jealous of his honor and not to be trifled with. Sempronio and Pármeno, looking through the lens of fear see an ogre whose home is a fortress manned by well-fed and well-armed servants who desire nothing so much as a fight (act XIII). Thought of Pleberio's wrath is enough to make even Celestina stop and hesitate in her tracks (act IV). The social presence of the parents (especially the father) is felt as an aura or projection and is powerfully developed by rumor and hearsay. Such is what is *expected* of a wealthy and noble father who has an only daughter.

Their second function is to oppose a kind of small, intimate, and futile counterplot to the principal thrust of events. The mother and father plan their daughter's future and talk about marriage; at their age anything could happen, and daughter and property might be parted. It is never too early, the aged Pleberio says (Act XVI), to take thought for the morrow and hedge fortune and the various hostile forces of the wicked world. The dramatic irony is almost too much as Pleberio lists the desirable qualities which make her the most marriageable girl in the city: money, status, modesty, virginity; and then Alisa says not to be hasty, Melibea is a little girl, so sheltered that any mention of a man would startle her. This counterplot is not restricted to what mother and father in their benign ignorance propose for their daughter, but it includes the whole domestic scene, the reality against which Calisto and Celestina have conspired. The imagined severity does not exist; there is no heavy father inviting rebellion, no forbiddingly vigilant mother provoking duplicity. They are not model parents, either in their intelligence or in their understanding of their daughter's needs, perhaps. They could have concerned themselves more directly with her, spent less time on making money, left her less in the care of servants, and so on (i.e., the familiar criticisms). It is easy for us, as amateur psychologists, to see where they went wrong. But Melibea is Melibea, and it is perhaps hard on the parents to suggest that her road to hell is paved with their good intentions. Nothing in her upbringing can explain her rebellious itch to us: why she wanted the furtive excitement of being seduced by Calisto in the dark but not married to him in the light of day. Only some rather old-fashioned words like original sin can do that. And if she had decided to marry, everything points to the reasonable certainty that she would have been allowed to choose Calisto.

Thus, the private, domestic view of the parents inspires not fear and respect but pathos and pity. They are remote and ineffectual, not the ogres written into Calisto's and his servants' private melodrama. Desire projects infantile fantasies onto the offended parties (but it sees clearly enough *who* they are and that they truly are offended). If they are foolish, well-meaning, credulous, and inattentive (as indeed they are; Alisa's flippant unconcern about Celestina's visit shocks Lucrecia), they are still enittled to ask, like the parents of other teenage children, "why does this happen to me?" It can be argued, without prejudice to what has just been said, however, that this counterplot is opposed to the events only at the surface level of the action. At the deeper level of the play, where all the action is rooted in concepts of the insufficiency of human nature and the reality of evil, plot and counterplot share a common source and direction. For this reason, I defer analysis of Pleberio's final speech (act XXI) to chapter 8.

CHAPTER 7

# *Structures*

## I *General*

WORKS of art may be articulated in numerous different ways. On looking at a painting by, say, Van Gogh we may find that the way the paint is applied gives a characteristic shape and energy to the whole, before we even begin to analyze its subject. Or we may notice that color-masses set up patterns of attraction and repulsion between one another, rather like fields of force. Different kinds of significance may adhere to the center or to the periphery, to objects in isolation or in groups, to patterns or to random distribution, according to the composition chosen by the painter. In older paintings iconography may be important; that is to say, a scheme of conventional meanings assigned to particular objects in given situations. We know from this kind of convention that a lady seated under a gold canopy, dressed in blue and holding a baby whose hand is raised, will be a "Virgin and Child"; that an old ragged gentleman with a long beard sitting by a grotto, with a rock in his hand, is St. Jerome. There are, admittedly, occasions for confusion: a burly man carrying a club may be Hercules, but he could also be Christ rescuing Adam from Limbo. Allegories present problems of identification also: are those three female figures the three Graces or the theological virtues, Faith, Hope and Charity? But the point at issue here is that as we go back in time, we move further and further away from a basic assumption of modern art, that the materials and the techniques of the artist can be their own, self-sufficient subject.

Scenes from classical or biblical history, and allegories (which are means of representing ideas, or metaphorical reconstructions, of human belief and value) predominate into the Renaissance. Even with eighteenth-century landscapes, one is often uncertain whether the artist is representing a particular scene or symbolizing the world through a visual metaphor of harmony and balance and glowing serenity. Thus it is only in comparatively recent times that European art has ceased to use nonvisual subjects—religious, moral, philosophical, historical—around which to organize the visual experience. And history was nothing if not exemplary. The visual arts derived their values from those areas of life from which individuals and society largely derived them. Yet the greatest painters have been those who did not embody the greatest quantity of moral or religious significance, but those who, organizing this nonvisual conceptual material in terms of color, mass, distribution, tensions, and distances, thought it through in their materials and techniques.

It can be dangerous to proceed by analogy from one art to another, but the advantage in this case is that, just as in the example of painting, we see the distinction that exists between (1) the material means (both the stuff and the action) by which it is achieved; (2) the virtual space within which relationships are organized; and (3) the nonvisual source of the subject and its value; so in literature (1) and (3) are separate, though to the inexperienced reader they look identical. Words communicate, we are told, and the medium is the message.[1] However, the message is, as we see, the "nonart" component, the derived part which can be paraphrased and reduced to statement or message or moral, and in fact the same message could be repeated by an infinite number of works of art—good, bad, and mediocre. Literature uses words (1) and words have established meanings (3). But the author is no more speaking the meanings of the words he uses than the painter is depicting "what really happened" at the Last Supper. From him the significance is in (2), namely, the particular structure which this work of art, and no other, has.

To conclude this preamble, absurdly brief as it is, I want particularly to make two points clear. First, that as a matter of historical fact, old literature, like old paintings, is organized around something (story, history, moral) which can only be authenticated, if at all, outside the work itself. We must not treat it as the whole work, or as what makes art art, but neither should we go to the other extreme and deny that it is there as a legitimate condition of the work's existence. Second, the par-

ticular form and structure of the work of art give it its unique
value as an experience; not the fact of the Lord's Supper or a
smiling Mona Lisa but the vision of these events, by which
Lisa, for instance, is felt to be *gioconda* in an unrepeatable but
eternalized moment. Structure is the patterns set up in the
mind, the implicit grammar, syntax, and vocabulary of the work's
meaning. In this chapter we shall observe the signs on which
we shall base our conclusions in the next chapter, on "Meaning
and Vision."

## II  *Plot*

The oldest unit of structure that our critical vocabulary has
is *plot*. This is not the same as the *action,* the "what-people-do-
and-say," but the way the action is organized. When we are not
thinking about what we are saying we may use "plot" to mean
"action," but even so we tacitly acknowledge that it is not the
action in the same form as it might have appeared in a news-
paper, a history book, a film, or the record of a trial. Plot is the
action *arranged* for narrating, or the action *arranged* for acting,
according to whether we are dealing with a novel or a play.
But if it is the action told for the form's (novel's, play's) sake,
it is also the action told for significance's sake. Some plots are
told from the beginning, others backward, from the end, others
start in the middle and make us look both ways. The perspective
on events is different in each case, and perspective is as much
part of the meaning of a literary work as it is of a visual one.
A plot may follow a close sequence of events, or a single event
in minute detail, or bring together episodes widely separated
in time or space. A life, the fortunes of a family, a city, a people,
may be shaped into a novel or an epic. The repertory of actions
and events is constantly repeated; but the range of plots is
limitless.

*La Celestina* has a simple story: "he" falls in love with "her"
and it all turns out horribly in the end. There are not many
variations on this basic story or action. Lovers are either happily
united or they are not. They may be first one then the other,
through many twists and turns, but the outcome has to be one or
the other, romance or tragedy, except for those few occasions

when (as in the film *Brief Encounter*) they stoically separate in recognition of a duty, or truth to themselves. So *La Celestina* gives the lovers a brief run of joy (a single night in the *Comedia*, a month or more in the *Tragicomedia*) before the catastrophe. At this level of analysis, the book is not unusual, since the formal closure is usually a death or a wedding (or a symbolic death like Miss Haversham's petrification of her past in Dickens' *Great Expectations*). This is another testimony to the unreality of literature. If we look for mirrorlike fidelity to ordinary experience we shall be deceived, for births, weddings, and deaths are the ritual points of significance in life, not the content of everyday routine. Statistically, they count for little compared to the miles we drive, the meals we eat, the diapers we change, or the futile, frustrating, insignificant things we do as part of our work and (if we are fortunate and healthy) promptly forget. In literature, certain situations have value because they help us organize our response to the fiction world, rather than because they are socially required. It so happens that in the real world most happy couples do eventually marry. If couples in a novel or a play also marry, this does not mean that the author is making propaganda for marriage or that marriage is the message or that he is being a social and religious conformist. Rather, it is likely to mean that the permanence of a relationship is being symbolically rendered. It is the desire for order, harmony, and stability which the act embodies, rather than conformity with the institution as it is in real life. Thus far, it is obvious that the sequence of deaths in *La Celestina* and the rejection of marriage will have to be accommodated as two aspects of the same meaning.

There are some notable peculiarities in the way Rojas has plotted his story. The large number of deaths (five) in a small cast of characters puts it on a level with *Hamlet* for a story of "carnal, bloody, and unnatural acts" (act V, scene 2). The persons who die are all connected with the action, and the logic of art (which from Homer to G. B. Shaw is the logic of final causes) requires that we look for a point of diffusion. At that point, certain irrevocable choices of ends and means are made. The very simplicity, unity, and connectedness of the action will make it difficult to sustain a view of these events as coincidence, as randomness, as a cosmic indifference to man, which we twentieth-century post-Christian readers could find emotionally satisfying. The story of *Celestina* is disposed in such a way that the beginning is unmistakably located in the personal encounter of Calisto with Melibea. Once that encounter has taken place, Calisto has only one purpose—to have Melibea—and here again there are no diversionary interests in his life. His whole being is concentrated upon that single goal. The other characters who appear in the story are all instrumental to that end though, naturally, they have their own interests to serve. If these interests become baser as the circle of involvement grows larger, this fact may contribute to the terms in which we evaluate the center of that circle—Calisto and his passion. Beside Calisto stand his two servants who have turned predators, and beyond them the meretricious world of prostitutes. This latter, we may observe, is not put there in order to be sentimentally explained away by future generations, but to symbolize the reality of evil in the confusion of men's appetites.

Two more facts can be added to this preliminary inventory of characteristics of the plot. They are obvious ones, but in thinking about art, nothing is ever too obvious to have significance. First, there is no hero, in even the most general meaning of that word. Calisto might be called the protagonist or principal character, for the reasons that the action originates in his desire, culminates in the satisfaction of his desire, and destroys itself in the consequences of his desire. But straight away we see that Calisto and the action are ruled by his desire and not the other way about. His passivity earns him no emotional sympathy. Apart from Melibea, who realizes that she has everything to lose, and accepts this as a fact of love, only her parents invite sympathy. The parents, however, cannot be said to elicit more than a marginal pathos; they are too insignificant, their unawareness is too incongruous. Melibea is conscious of their feelings, but they are never conscious of hers. Pleberio's final claim to our attention (act XXI) is too plaintively concerned with the collapse of his personal world and expectations for us to feel that he can conciliate our desire for some positive word in all this disarray.

Some readers accept Pleberio as a hero by default. On this

view, he represents the final intellectual viewpoint of the play: a world indifferent to man where, as Gloster says in *King Lear* "As flies to wanton boys are we to the gods / They kill us for their sport." Here I would like to measure his role rather than evaluate the content of his speech. It is appropriate to observe, then, that he is the only character who has done nothing, has experienced none of the action, has been disconnected from everyone else, and therefore has no credentials for appearing as an Everyman or a chorus. Spokesmen who step forward to address the audience at the end of the play, whether in medieval moralities or the modern political moralities, have to be either principal characters or wise observers who see the whole play. Pleberio, on the contrary, has shrunk in dramatic status from the feared patrician (in the mind of Calisto and Celestina) and the night ogre (in the stark fantasies of the servants) to an ineffectual parent who cannot see beyond his nose, who yields to his more foolish wife. He has been given a role of unassuming minor absurdity behind the social mask: the closer we approach him, the more of a mediocrity he appears. His is one of the few expressive names in the cast, Pleberio clearly denoting vulgarity. To award the dignity of a revelation, a manifestation of the world's real moral nature to a character who is disparaged in the mere fact of being brought into focus, would constitute a serious discontinuity, a structural incoherence, in the fabric of the *Celestina.* This would invalidate whatever interpretation one were to put upon him. Whatever dignity or tenderness Pleberio has is created for us more by Melibea's guilty and sorrowful expressions of love for him than by his for her. If we take Pleberio as Rojas gives him to us—an aging man now looking out on his life of accumulation and investment, and becoming aware that he has a daughter, who will inherit it all, who must therefore be married, because men will try to take advantage of her, etc.—we may begin to see his place in the grimly ironic structure of events. Let us, for a start, then, assume that Rojas is consistent and that Pleberio's monologue reveals, not a "Godless natural universe"[2] but the soul of an entrepreneur. Melibea gambled everything on her love for Calisto, this life and the next. Her gambler's throw is more awesome and appalling than Pleberio's lifetime of careful investment, and, being more absolute, it is ultimately more tragic in its power to suspend judgment. Inevitably, the positive feelings of a person in that state of final desperation carry conviction, and from the last words of Melibea we see that Pleberio is not unloved. The delicate pathos of this situation, I believe, would be overwhelmed by taking the puzzlement of Pleberio in act XXI (which is in keeping with what I have called his "disconnectedness") and claiming that it represents Rojas' own metaphysical doubts.[3]

The second obvious point (the first was that there is no hero, no stable protagonist, and no character with whom to identify sympathetically) is that Celestina acquires a position of immense influence in the action. Yet her relation to the plot is ambiguous. Calisto is in love with Melibea, and Melibea, as she confesses (act XII), has struggled in vain to suppress her feelings for him. It would seem that some more direct and economical way might be found to bring them together than for Sempronio to solicit Celestina, Celestina to invoke Pluto, then corrupt Pármeno, and for the three of them to die. It no doubt occurred to Rojas, as it has done to innumerable readers, that if Calisto had asked her father for her hand in marriage, he might have had little difficulty. Some critics have asked why he did not go to Pleberio, what was the social impediment? and have provided answers which excel in ingenuity (as usually is the case when the question itself is unnecessary).[4] The fact is that there is no impediment to marriage, and by making it clear that Melibea loves him, that the difference of lineage and fortune is relative, and that her father is willing to allow her the choice (act XVI), Rojas gives the lovers (and Calisto especially) the responsibility for choosing the tortuous, illicit, and dangerous route to fulfillment. In making this choice, personal responsibility is at once abdicated first onto Sempronio and then onto Celestina, who is made the mover of events. She becomes the center, the point from which all energy radiates, and also the vortex into which individual desires are drawn. So while it is true that Celestina is not organically necessary,[5] in the sense that everything is already disposed in the lovers' favor, she is necessary as the embodiment of their desires on the level of evaluation. As an outward projection of the evil that is within, she may be compared to the disintegrating portrait of Dorian Gray, in Oscar Wilde's story.

More dubious in its structural necessity is Celestina's invocation of Pluto (act III). The matter cannot be settled by asking whether people in the 1490s believed in witchcraft and in communication with the devil. The answer, as one would expect, is that many persons did believe in the possibility of both, but that many of those who believed that it was possible to summon the devil were skeptical of the claims of self-styled witches to have achieved it. So we are back with the text, and we may recall that Pármeno, who was brought up by her, and whose mother was also a witch, says "it was all tricks and lies" (act I; I, 86). Celestina's sincerity or insincerity is not to the point, though in her behalf it may be said that she is alone, is not trying to impress anyone with her powers, and that Elicia, who has helped her get the necessary ingredients together, takes it all for granted, without comment. (Like other superstitious believers, she prays when in need, but attributes successes to her own energy and experience.) But the devil's hand is never shown, Celestina claims the credit for herself in Melibea's surrender, Pármeno's surrender is engineered without any such request for diabolical aid, and (as we noted) Melibea confesses that she loved Calisto from the beginning. So the question of the efficacy of Celestina's command to Pluto is not susceptible of any realistic evidence. The act is not to be evaluated for what it does in a causal sequence, but for what it indicates about the significance of other acts, the reality of evil implicit in choices already made.

In discussing the characters in the last chapter, we observed Rojas' practice of pairing, and that each pairing contained similarities and contrasts, positions and counterpositions. Within the plot, two notable pairings can be found: Celestina's two triumphs (over Pármeno and Melibea) and the two scenes of lovemaking in Melibea's garden. In passing we can state what the reader has by this time discovered for himself: that the different aspects of structure cannot be neatly separated from one another. As in a three-dimensional game of chess, one can view the vertical planes or the horizontal ones, but each pattern has implications in the other planes and makes connections between them. So Celestina's seduction of Pármeno advances the action in the direction she requires and makes him a member of the team which is dedicated to satisfying, and fleecing, Calisto. At the same time, it is a sample of Celestina's skill, in anticipation of her success with Melibea. It stresses the purely natural means she uses—depth psychology, substitution, and transference—and shows how evil works with the normal desires and insecurities of individuals. It also does something quite different to the plan of the whole work, which is clear in the *Comedia* but obscured by the *Tragicomedia*; namely, it bisects the whole action. Celestina leaves Pármeno in bed with Areusa at the end of act VII, and in act VIII he rises late, sees that it is already midmorning, goes back to Calisto's lodging, and finds Sempronio waiting, sardonic and ready to take sweet revenge on this self-righteous youth who has opposed all their plans. But it is the "new" Pármeno who comes to greet him, to seek an ear for his last night's escapade, and to pledge friendship. This new Pármeno risen from the ashes of the old, enters at the mathematical midpoint of the original sixteen acts. It is a watershed, a point beyond which nothing is the same as before. It seals the fate, not only of Pármeno himself, but of everyone else. It strengthens Celestina's hold on Calisto, and gives Sempronio an ally against Celestina (a result which she had not expected). From this point, the apex of the structure, there is a downhill momentum as everything—relationships, values—is overturned (a *catastrophe* in the original Greek sense).

Originally, in the *Comedia,* there was only one love scene; the duplication was added in the *Tragicomedia.* It will be more economical, therefore, to study this particular duplication as part of the comparison of the two versions, which follows in the next section.

### III   Comedia *and* Tragicomedia

The principal change from *Comedia* to *Tragicomedia* is the addition of five new acts. Originally, Calisto fell from his ladder (in act XIV) shortly after enjoying Melibea for the first and only time. The sixteen-act form, as we have just seen, put the corruption of Pármeno at the halfway point, thus emphasizing that "the good" (in the form of Pármeno's loyalty) is what stands in the way of Calisto's pleasure and, conversely, that his gratification is bought by the corruption of others. The disasters occur with great rapidity in the final few acts: Melibea gives her consent to Celestina (act X) who tells Calisto; Elicia prophesies a fall (act XI); after the night meeting at Melibea's door, Sempronio and Pármeno kill Celestina (act XII); Calisto learns the news of the deaths (act XIII) and physically seduces Melibea that same night and falls to his own death (act XIV). Thus, after eleven acts of talk, persuasion, prevarication, bribery, despair, crumbling loyalties, and betrayals (the duration of Celestina's ascendancy) the physical disasters ensue. All the deaths occur in a span of scarcely more than three acts, and twenty-four hours of imagined time. A sense of continual shock is sustained from the moment of Melibea's "yes" to Calisto until the end of the play.

Perhaps Rojas was not joking when he wrote, in the prologue, that friends persuaded him to enlarge the play and extend the course of the lovers' pleasures ("el processo de su deleyte destos amantes"; I, 26). If he undertook it unwillingly ("contra mi voluntad"), however, there is nothing half-hearted about the execution, for the earlier acts are also added to, with a meticulous sense of style. The new block of action consists of a monologue by Calisto on the change in his fortunes (act XIV); Areusa's and Elicia's recoveries from the deaths of Celestina and their lovers, and their plan to use Centurio (a new character) to gain revenge on Calisto (acts XV, XVII, XVIII); Sosia's gullible fascination with Areusa who wants information from him (act XVII); Alisa's and Pleberio's discussion of the need to get Melibea married (act XVI); a second more extended, lyrically intense love scene than the first (act XIX). What Rojas has given us in these additions is a new structure which delays the catastrophe, or, more correctly, delays the completion of it, since the deaths of Celestina, Sempronio, and Pármeno have already taken place and begun the sequence which yet has to be formally completed in the deaths of the lovers.

Perhaps the most obvious effect of the new section is to reveal how each character accepts the deaths of the others. No one pauses to say "There but for the grace of God go I," or any other appropriate phrase, and this is highly significant in that age which made of death so clear and ominous a judgment upon life. Holbein, in his painting *The Ambassadors* (1533), has placed a curious shape whose meaning is not revealed until the painting is observed as it would have been seen in its original location—on a stairway. There, from the viewpoint of the person descending the stairs, the tilted and elongated shape would be foreshortened and reveal a skull, a Death's head, the familiar *memento mori*. The ambassadors of the title are richly dressed, confident, powerful in the full flush of youth. And that, as anyone who ever read the Psalms or Ecclesiastes or St. Paul or a host of latter-day writers knows, is the most thoughtless state; the gilded youth would care least about death and consequently were in the most dangerous state of mind. Montaigne, not noted for excessive piety, writes of the care we should have not to judge anyone happy until the moment of his death, and he quotes Lucretius' lines about death snatching off the mask and exposing the reality.[6] But fortune and death, such powerful allies, awake no echoes in Calisto or Melibea. There are many places in *La Celestina* where the characters cite phrases from Petrarch about changing fortune, but these are idle words on idle lips. Elicia's mourning yields quickly to the urge to resume her life. There are many lovers around the door of Areusa (including the cowardly braggart Centurio), and her desire for revenge is more an appetite of her personality than the reflex of love for the departed Pármeno, or of respect for Celestina, whose overbearing protectiveness she is happy to escape. Calisto and Melibea, in their bower of bliss, mention nothing so unpleasant as death. Calisto's own reflections (acts XIII, XIV), are concerned with how his reputation will be affected and how to conceal the chain of events from public view (see commentary on acts XIII, XIV). His easy way of dissociating himself from those whom he no longer needs has been called "odious" (Lida, *Originalidad* p. 350). His shift from the unpleasant memories to erotic fantasies has been sharply observed by Gilman:

Rojas is trying to tell us just this: the sense of Calisto's anguish, his sudden concern for honor and for the death of his servants comes— and can only come—at a time when his desire has been satisfied. The great monologue of act XIV, perhaps the greatest achievement of the additions, was possible only on the morning after the night of love. Both Rojas and Calisto know it; both know that the release from amorous urgency has exposed an underlying ugliness.[7]

Today, we underline the importance of death by avoiding the subject, and by making it expensive. Formerly, and in Latin countries even now, death was talked about, witnessed, anticipated, made a communal experience. That is why it is so astonishing that no one talks about it in *La Celestina*. Until, that is, we remember the private worlds into which all these characters have withdrawn themselves.

Under the shadow of these deaths, Calisto and Melibea continue their idyll. Their garden of delights is on a plateau where the unwary foot will discover the next drop into catastrophe. Under the shadow of these deaths, Elicia and Areusa prosper and glitter as never before. The additions extend the time of the action so that we can see Celestina's world, without Celestina. What was she, without her genius for selling, her incitements and persuasions (for which Calisto and Melibea give her no credit after the event), but a repellent bag of memories, of nostalgia for her former glories? So Calisto and Melibea enjoy their artificial paradise, thinking that the serpent is dead. As for Areusa, she has her own glories, now. The world has not changed because Celestina departed.

The absence of Celestina and the extension of time allows the lovers to float on sensuality and fantasy in the illusion that time has stopped. Perhaps this perception owes some of its force to the fact that we know—our modern editions tell us—when the additions begin and end. Nevertheless, Melibea's songs (act XIX), her joy in anticipation which is almost greater than her pleasure of fulfillment, and Calisto's avoidance of the light of day are signs of a state of mind so highly charged with unreality that the first contact with ground will be fatal. Calisto has had more than a month in which to know the mettle of his new valets. "Cómo se desasna!" ("How smart he's become!") exclaims Elicia on hearing Sosia talk (II, 168). But Calisto rushes unnecessarily to their help and does not wait to feel for the ladder before coming down off the wall.

In this period of distended time, everything is changing (Eli-

cia will move in with Areusa, Celestina is being forgotten, Sosia
is growing up, Areusa is beginning to hold glamorous court,
Pleberio and Alisa talk about Melibea's future); everything
changes except the lovers' escapes into their private heaven. It
is now that the two counterplots are set moving. Pleberio wants
Melibea to marry; Areusa wants Centurio to kill Calisto. Both
schemes fail, because the originators are blind. Pleberio does
not see Melibea; Areusa (so proud in her manipulation of little
Sosia) is fooled by the biggest fool, Centurio. The theme of
not seeing, of being wise in one's own conceit, is continued
through the additions, fragmented and replayed in new formal
patterns.

The other additions, which are to be found throughout the
play, affect the plot in small, subtle ways which it would be
impossible to detail in a book of this nature. They vary from
single words, a "you" or the name of the person addressed, which
minutely intensifies the speaker-listener relation, to extensive
paragraphs of reminiscence or rhetorical exclamation. To put it
generally, Rojas has become more experienced in the art of
dialogue and in sustaining the point of view of each speaker,
as well as that speaker's awareness of himself and his listener
and the structure of their relation at each moment of utterance.
Some editors and commentators dismiss the additions as the work
of a hack who botched Rojas' *Comedia*. Gilman (*The Art*) brilliantly justified the changes. As he says, "So many of these lesser
changes . . . betray such an evidently stylistic preoccupation. . . .
Only a person creatively aware of each line could have made
them or would have thought it worth while to do so" (p. 16).

## IV  *Causality*

In the simple story of *La Celestina* it is not difficult to perceive
the chain of cause and effect, the logic of events. From the
moment when Calisto's hawk enters (by accident or Calisto's
design, we cannot tell) Melibea's garden, the dependence of
all further action on his passion is clear. From Calisto's not
taking the road to marriage, the world of Celestina becomes
the seamy side of Calisto's high-sounding desires, and the way
of secrecy, tension, risk, and hasty misjudgment is opened. The

action is basically simple and tight and proceeds in rigorous sequence. One thing follows closely after another, scenes are knit into one another without break, nothing of consequence happens that we are not witness to, nothing is reported by messengers or eyewitnesses, except the execution of Sempronio and Pármeno.

Around this simple story is a vast tissue of circumstantial detail. What is not given by the plot is derived convincingly from character, from the opportunities of the moment, or from the psychological state of the speaker at the particular instant and in the particular relation in which he stands to another character. A case in point is the summoning of Celestina into Calisto's affairs. She is not indispensable in the light of Melibea's secret love for Calisto. Her principal function is to resolve the conflict between desire and honor in Melibea. Without her, some plot could be formed. But it would be a different plot, and the one that does follow from Celestina's actions is, for all its simplicity, an intricate web of personal feelings and responses to immediate situations. When Calisto goes home after hearing Melibea's rude rebuff he plunges into despair. His servant Sempronio debates whether to go into his room or not, as cowardice and self-interest compete within him. In Calisto's presence he assumes an attitude of superior worldliness laced with morality. He also makes jokes, disparages women, and tries the kind of speech that servants are expected to use, urging him to fortitude, and to consider how well endowed he is by nature and fortune, so that he will be loved by all. Only when Calisto persists in his desire does Sempronio offer to fetch Celestina in order, he says, "to save you from despair" (I, 57). This decision, then, arises from the character of Sempronio who is unwilling to listen any more to Calisto's ravings, has lost his own patience, and, in any case, is not blessed with the qualities of a counselor. Strength of mind, integrity, and firmness of character are not to be found in him, and as he flits from one recourse to another, not caring about self-contradiction but trying what will work, Rojas shows us that he is the disastrously right servant for such a master. Calling Celestina will get Calisto off his own back, but he will still be able (he hopes) to get some fat commission, as the gift Calisto has just given him seems to promise. Thus

Celestina, who (as we saw above) makes this plot what it is, and whose presence reveals so much about the weaknesses of everyone else, is brought in on the perfectly understandable impulse of a secondary character.

Another instance of a lesser character serving the writer's larger purposes is provided by Pármeno. Judged in objective terms of the economy of the action, there is no reason for him to become so important. As an obstacle to Celestina and Sempronio, carping and making sarcastic remarks about "an old painted whore" and presenting unwelcome home truths like "you lost your freedom when you gave up your will" (I, 122), Pármeno is a nuisance but not an impediment and could be removed if necessary. But the plot gains from his being seduced by Celestina, and if this event is not essential to Calisto, it facilitates that part of the action which leads to Celestina's own destruction. It gains in dramatic irony too, since Celestina is seen to be the source of her own ruin. But if Pármeno were circumvented, something would be missing from Celestina: her virtuosity would be by that much less well-attested, her response to a challenge "because it is there," her urge to sell, to capture clients, to make people her own, which is so effective a part of her rapacity—all this would be so much more weakly presented. She deals with him as she does, not so much because it is directly necessary to the action, but because that is *her* way, and this fuller definition of Celestina is necessary to the plot.

There are secondary causalities also, which once again are firmly tied to character or circumstance. Arriving at Melibea's house, Celestina could scarcely have expected that the mother, Alisa, would be so unconcerned at her presence or that she would almost immediately leave the house to visit a sick sister (act IV). The next time (act X), Alisa warns her daughter against having dealings with the old woman (II, 65), which provokes Lucrecia's comments "The mistress is waking up too late." This dithering between careless trust and ineffectual admonition, between laughter at Lucrecia's discomfort on meeting Celestina and tight-lipped call for modesty, is inconsistent behavior, but artistically appropriate when it originates in a light-headed and disorganized personality. Her later insistence that her daughter is too innocent to talk of marriage (act XIV) completes this personality, who is as removed from reality in her way as Calisto is in his. In this lack of a parental mind we can see a secondary causality which Alisa shares with Pleberio. Neither is an incitement to Melibea, obviously, and they do not constitute a repression which provokes rebellion in her. Their fault is simply a failure to see, to recognize, to know people for what they are, and to prevent dangerous occasions.

## V  Structures of Irony

There are in *La Celestina* an uncountable number of dramatic ironies, moments when the reader is aware of something and the character is not, or when the reader perceives that the character is working against what he is striving to attain. Pleberio discussing with Alisa the need for Melibea to marry, praising her virginity and modesty (which she has so recently surrendered)—and all this within range of Melibea's hearing—is a fine example. In itself though, it indicates a local limitation of vision, even if it interacts with other local ironies, as for example, Lucrecia's muddled envy and censure of Melibea. And we must be prepared to ask whether Pleberio's final oration is the last of the great failures of perception, as I implied earlier in this chapter (section II). Celestina's corruption of Pármeno makes him an ally, but it leads to her own final undoing. Ironies, then, may get larger and larger to encompass whole segments of the action. The largest are those in which the whole plot is perceived differently by those who are in it than by those who are spectators. Here one may reasonably speak of irony as structure, since it serves to separate planes of perception and thus to articulate meaning in the point of view of the spectator who is outside the action looking in. We may look for it in certain recurrent or tenaciously present images, or implied images.

The first such image is that of "the world upside down" (*el mundo al revés*).[8] Such a notion is familiar to us in specific images of reversal in the language of prophecy: "The wolf also shall dwell with the lamb, and the leopard shall lie down with the kid; and the calf and the young lion and the fatling together; and a little child shall lead them" (Isaiah 11:6); "But many that are first shall be last and the last shall be first" (Matthew 19:30). Prophecy assures us, in language like this, that the inequities of this world will be reversed or that the kingdom of God will, happily, not be like the kingdom of men. The implication, then, is that the world of mankind has reversed the proper orders and values: the world we live in is the really upside-down one.[9] The traditional Feast of Fools, the revels of the Lord of Misrule, the ceremony of the Boy Bishop, all upended the accepted order of things for a day, by deposing the figures who, for three hundred and sixty-four days command authority and reverence, and making them subject to someone who is normally despised. ("He hath put down the mighty from their seats . . ." [Luke I:51].) Christ himself conformed to this pattern; the "King of Kings" is a lamb, a child, an outcast, who conquers by dying and promises that service is freedom. The literary applications of this topic are manifold. The distempered mind of Hamlet sees the fair world in a series of loathesome images (*Hamlet*, act II, scene 2), and the Witches foresee murder and tyranny on the throne of Scotland, with the refrain "Fair is foul, and foul is fair" (*Macbeth*, act I, scene 1). In these examples, an idea of goodness or truth or justice or order is travestied, and the travesty helps to guide the judgment of the reader or spectator. In *La Celestina* we see at the very beginning how the usual "God is love" has been inverted by the impassioned mind of Calisto into "love is God" and "Melibea is God." He pays to Melibea, and to his desire for her, the adoration and (in language at least) the cult and respect reserved for real religious devotion. This is partly derived (as we noted earlier) from a poetic tradition, but that does not weaken the individual case, especially when it is in combination with so many other compatible images. He so far loses control of his judgment that he uses this language of religious exaltation to Celestina: "O jewel of the world, easer of pain . . ."; "My glory and my comfort. . . ." The lofty image of Melibea is in turn inverted by Elicia and Areusa, as they quarrel with Sempronio at the banquet (act IX) and compete in finding repulsive epithets for her:

AREUSA. God forgive me, but if you were to meet her on an empty stomach, you'd be off your food for the rest of the day. She

shuts herself up all year with packs made from all kinds of filth. If she ever goes out where she can be seen she loads her face with gall and honey and bread poultices and dried figs and other things that I won't mention at table. It's their money that gets the likes of her all the praise for being beautiful, not their attractive bodies. I swear, for a virgin she's got breasts that look as if she'd had three children— they're big as pumpkins! I haven't seen her belly, but to judge from the rest of her I'd say it's as flabby as an old woman of fifty's. I don't know what Calisto sees in her. . . .
(II, 32–33)

When Sempronio appeals to the general reputation of Melibea's beauty, Areusa continues by assailing popular opinion, which is always the reverse of the truth,

Nothing is further from the truth than popular opinion. You'll never live happy if you follow the dictates of others. Whatever the crowd thinks is stupid, what it says is lies, what it censures is good, and what it praises, bad, and that's the honest truth. . . . (II, 33–34)

Calisto from one side, and Areusa from the other, invert the norms of truth and beauty, on their different planes. From envy, Areusa makes beauty ugliness, whereas Calisto from idolatry makes the human divine. He elevates the material to the level of the spiritual, and worships it—but this does not prevent him from laying profane hands on it at the first opportunity.

Within this image of a world reversed, as in a frame, many other details will be seen to fit. Calisto retreats into the darkness, though he worships Melibea as a divine light. His way of life undoes the natural order of things, making day night and night day, and for this his servants regard him as crazy. As well they might, since conventional imagery links light with reason and darkness with passion and with ignorance, of which the willful kind is worst. Darkness is also diabolical, as light is angelic. Celestina herself, a peddler of artificial paradises, is thematically linked to Calisto as well as playing a formal part in the action. She specializes in the pleasures of the dark and has her own line of communication with the prince of darkness himself. Her name promises celestial rewards, and we have seen the irony of that. Everyone calls her "Mother," but what she gives is not life nor love. She "makes a man" of "her son" Pármeno by tapping his infantilism. Universal provider, what she gives destroys, and only she is enriched. Love has become a form of commerce. In act XI Calisto gives her the gold chain that so excites the envy of the servants. This is part of a reciprocal transaction in which Celestina is the broker, for the chain is given to her who had acquired Melibea's belt, an exchange rich in symbolic values. Earlier, she praises his magnificence *"in payment for which* I restore to you your health which was destroyed, your heart which was lost, your mind which was deranged" (II, 70). In the play, Pleberio is the prototype of the gold-getter who has neglected the human side of his relations, and it is part of Rojas' genius to reserve this surprise to the end. Thus the intricacies of the equation "love = commerce" are also part of this inverted world where human, spiritual, and social values are subjected to various manifestations of the grossly material.

Rojas' work is soaked in its literary origins, and we shall offer some brief references to these in the next chapter. Celestina's conjuring of Pluto is closely modeled on Lucan (*Pharsalia*, book VI), and the banquet may perhaps recall the one in Petronius' *Satyricon*, though unmannerly tables are not so unusual that a single model can be claimed. However, when the fictional world is also a critique of fiction, as it is in *La Celestina*, travesty may go beyond metaphors and puns and employ other fictions, of a more archetypal value. If Celestina claims Pármeno as her own child, brings him home from what she represents as his truancy of arrogant self-righteousness, and when the reunion is then celebrated with a banquet of stolen food, our recollection of the Prodigal Son's return may serve a purpose. Just as positive values—love, worship, service, etc.—may be turned upside down to reveal a topsy-turvy world, so universally recognized model fictions can be (and were) comically disfigured for the same purpose. Rojas, though, has gone further in tragicomic irony with his ending. When Melibea, the other wayward child, spends her treasure and then rejects her father, the travesty does not merely invert the happy comedy (in the medieval sense) of the parable. The model, symbolic of life and reconciliation, is rejected and destroyed. The artistic shock is equal to that of her suicide; indeed, the suicide is entirely consistent with it.

## VI    *Symbols*

As we stated at the beginning of this chapter, the assignment of specific meanings to particular objects in certain contexts is common in medieval and Renaissance art. With some modifications, the same may be said of literature.[10] When Hamlet, standing in an open grave, addresses Yorick's skull, we know immediately what is in his mind. Many such symbols are both pictorial and literary: "green" = hope, spring, rebirth; "sheep" = human soul; "outstretched hand" = trust, friendship; "cup" = spiritual communion, love; "serpent" = wisdom, but also perfidy and sin. The list is random, unsystematic, and of no significance in itself, except to show that, whereas the word "symbol" is now often used in a rather lax or abstruse way, medieval artists were more practical. Their symbols were a vocabulary with a one-to-one correspondence in any particular context, though later in the sixteenth century complex kinds of wit were formed from the interplay of visual emblems and verbal puns. Late medieval symbolism, however, aimed at clarity of exposition and would not tolerate any confusion of (say) the serpent of Apollo with that of Genesis.

In *La Celestina* a number of objects and acts have meanings which are evidently activated by the movement of events, the nature of the plot, and the context in which they are placed. Two recent essays in particular have focused attention on this matter, and the reader is referred to them for further details.[11] Briefly, since we shall be concerned with this matter again in chapter 8, we might note such well-confirmed symbols as "garden" = paradise; and "lady in a garden," or "lady in a tower" = lady enclosed in modesty or chastity. (Paintings show the Virgin Mary in a garden, virgin saints may be depicted in or beside a tower.) The belt also, naturally, signifies chastity (Melibea sends hers to Calisto, who treats it with improper rapture). In classical Roman comedy the belt (*zona*) has similar symbolic value. The ladder as a means of ascent to heaven (examples are found in the dreams of Jacob, St. Benedict, and St. Romuald) is parodied in Calisto's language of erotic fantasy. The persistence of the contrast light/dark, the vertical (or spirit-matter) axis of so much of the action, and the repeated motif of the fall, will already be familiar to the reader. Part of the function of the large structures is to coordinate the meanings which are implicit in just such motifs, symbols, images, and patterns as these.

# CHAPTER 8

## Meaning and Vision

IN discussing genre, characters, and structures in the preceding chapters, we have already indicated to a large degree the bearing they have upon the meaning, that is, how they are the medium of vision. This is unavoidable if what we have claimed is true, namely, that significance is in the disposition of the parts and in the many complex relations that are established among them. Consequently, the reader will necessarily encounter some repetition and recapitulation as we proceed to conclusions which have already been foreshadowed by earlier analysis. We begin with the explicit declaration of moral purpose in the book and then move on to the interrelation of the concepts of love, fortune, and death—the play's intellectual frame.

### I *Moralities*

The title of the book, as it appeared in editions later than that of 1499, is expanded into a statement of intent: "composed as a rebuke to those foolish lovers who are so carried away by their unbridled passions that they make their mistresses their God. Also, as a warning against the wiles of procuresses and wicked flattering servants." No one can deny that Calisto does act as just such a "foolish lover," for that note is struck at the very beginning. "Was any man lifted into glory in this life as I am now? The blessed saints themselves, who enjoy the heavenly vision, have no greater pleasure than I do in adoring you. . . . If God gave me a seat in heaven above his saints, I'd reckon myself less happy" (I, 32–33). And it does not need to be demonstrated that the wily procuress and the servants with their duplicity do exploit Calisto's weakness and lead him toward the catastrophe. However, these words are not a summary of the plot, but a guide to the proper response of the

147

reader. They define the book's hoped-for social effect. Now, there is no way of knowing whether these words were put there by Rojas, by Proaza, or by someone else at the printer's, so we cannot say that they represent the author's serious evaluation of his work. But supposing that they are by Rojas, are they a convincing statement of his intention as we see this intention realized in the work? The question is less easy to answer than appears at first sight.

It is scarcely likely that Rojas intended to reform his readers morally or to give foolish youths the prudence that they lack. No one would suggest that the value of a piece of literature is *verifiable* in the subsequent behavior of its readers, in the improvement or deterioration of their moral judgments. Only an extreme Platonist would wish to have the question framed in that form. Yet the questions of what a book does and should do to the reader recur in many variations including, of course, some specifically twentieth-century ones. The words of the title do convey the sense that *La Celestina* is an exploration of certain patterns of behavior and that the author has a moral attitude toward it which is transmitted to the public. We observed at the beginning of the last chapter that this part of the work of art, the "message," insofar as it can be formulated in words, is (like the historical or narrative element in a painting) something ambiguous. In itself, it can be expressed better in other terms, as the political lesson of *King Lear* can be better expounded in some other form without the distraction of a play. Nevertheless, it is *there* as a condition of the play's existence, as part of its human accessibility. It would be a narrow reading of *Macbeth* that discovered only a message about tyrants usurping royal authority (how many kings are there who can read and profit from it?) and a trivial one which responded to *Othello* by counseling us to choose advisers with care, not to believe gossip, and not to drop handkerchiefs. Yet it is true that each of these plays requires our judgment, our observation of ends and means, choices and their consequences, risks inherent in situations, gains and losses. We may not be able to extract a "lesson" or a "message" from such works without falsifying them, and this (paradoxical as it may seem) is even more apparent in literature which has firm doctrinal content, such as *A*

*Pilgrim's Progress*: that doctrine is the same as it would have been had Bunyan never written his great allegory of it. What matters in the reading is the experience of the doctrine in the appropriate imaginative terms, rather than the doctrine itself. Vaguer notions (current in the 1920s) about art "educating the sensibility" or "enhancing life" were testimony to a continuing desire to retain for the work of art a communicative, even an educative, function in relation to the public, as well as its expressive function in relation to the artist.

In the twentieth century, the decline of supernatural religions has accompanied (I do not say caused) a changed conception of the relations between persons. In the words of Octavio Paz,

nature has become a complex system of causal relations in which qualities disappear and are transformed into pure quantities; and his [modern man's] fellows have ceased to be fellows and are utensils, tools. Man's relation with nature and with his neighbour is not essentially different from that which he maintains with his automobile, his telephone, or his typewriter. In short, the grossest credulity —as seen in political myths—is the other side of the positive spirit. No one has faith, but everyone has illusions. But the illusions evaporate and then nothing is left but the void: nihilism and vulgarity.[1]

This quotation serves a double purpose: it defines an aspect of modern life, the culmination of a process of which Rojas witnessed the beginning. But more of that later. It also defines a society in which the only universally respected value is the grossest national product, in which art is judged by its price and the numbers of copies sold and is denied intrinsic worth. It has to be "redeemed," in the courtroom jargon, by a social value, whatever that may mean. One effect of this is that readers are bothered if they cannot immediately recognize the author's "purpose" (one does not pay good money for something which has no purpose), and consequently they ask the question that so enraged Vladimir Nabokov: "What's the guy trying to say?"[2] The other effect is that if the author (Rojas, for example) does say what his "purpose" was, and he expresses it in moral or religious terms, there are many readers who will refuse to believe him. There is, then, a confusion between belief and history, that is, a tendency to disregard, even to reject, the religious orientation of writers of the past and to discover atheism in writers whose religion was not spread out in plain view. We cannot say too often that the world of the characters is not that of the author.

The desire that the author declare his intention represents one way in which the relation between author and public has not changed. The kind of intention which the public expects is what has changed. If Rojas did not give a summary of *La Celestina* which pleases modern readers, we should bear two contradictory thoughts in mind. First, every artist knows that he cannot convey his "intention" except through the expressive power of the work itself. Second, it is precisely on the human content of the work that the public will most readily and easily judge him, as we know from recent history (public rejection of post-Impressionism and Expressionism, for example; and the official rejection in Russia of nonrepresentational formalism). The kind of intention expressed by *La Celestina's* extended title recognizes a necessary relation between author and public, one which he shared with medieval writers generally as well as with many later authors. The essence of this relation is the perception of a truth or complex of truths which they hold in common. It was not the writer's business to reveal himself, to expose the contents of his subconscious mind, or to be unique in some way, but to reexpress with new force and insight mankind's ever-changing, ever-renewed sense of old truths. Not truths in the form of propositions or statements; not truths, that is to say, which people can hold, which the mind can contain, but truths which hold people and which sustain minds. Man's relation to God, nature, time, death, and an order in the universe—these are the form of such truths.

We may refer at this point to two phrases by two influential medieval writers. The first, by Alexander of Hales (d. 1245) stated that "learning looks toward understanding, as art looks toward action."[3] This opposition and clear demarcation of intellect and action, knowing and doing, rules out many of the post-Romantic claims for art, for example, that it is a cognitive act, a mystical experience, a contemplation of beauty, etc. The artist sees the world as it is already known and imitates some part of its operation. If he is successful, the person who contemplates it will be moved to good acts—assuming, of course, that he uses his understanding as the artist used his. The other statement, by St. Thomas Aquinas, complements the first at the point we have just reached: "the value of art is seen not in the artist but rather in the work itself."[4] Not in the intention of the artist, not in the emotional response of the spectator or reader, but in the qualities of the work as it is. And this means that the spectator or reader uses his judgment in evaluating what he sees. He knows if a work is good by using his rational faculty—the same that will tell him whether or not acts are good also. Art, then, exercises the same faculty that people use in order to choose their acts and judge those of other persons. But this is not to say that good artists have to be good men; nor that a fool will perform sensible acts as a consequence of experiencing good art.

There is thus no need to reject the declaration of the title of *La Celestina* as being wholly alien to Rojas' artistry. But if it is not alien, it is not essential either, because it looks to how the work might be justified rather than to what it is. This says merely what has been implied in the last three chapters, that *La Celestina* addresses the reader through its moral vision rather than through persuasion, exhortation, or awful warnings. But, it has been objected, the book is full of moralities, wise sayings, proverbs, and the like, which do not point to a moral end; far from it, they are put into the mouths of characters who use them in order to persuade other characters to actions which contrast outrageously with the tenor of the phrase.[5] Celestina is the greatest user of moral sayings, which she addresses both to others and to herself, in order to strengthen her resolve. And there are contradictory generalities in these dialogues. But, as Professor Fraker observed, the misuse that a character makes of philosophical or moral assertions need not deprive them of their independent value. "Totally 'non-realistic' doctrinal works in which this occurs are legion."[6] It is the exemplary action which points up the truth or falsehood of the assertions.[7] Similarly with the famous "realism" of the book: "one conclusion that could be drawn from all this evidence (Fraker continues) is precisely that verism is *not* the organizing principle in the *Celestina*, but rather the enunciation of theme, the *reprobatio amoris*, and that the whole stuff of the drama, complex as it is, 'realistic' as much of it is, is really at the service of this enunciation."

Before closing this discussion of the didactic claims which have been made for *La Celestina* (surely the least interesting aspect of it), we should consider the "immorality" of the actions that take place. It is usually assumed that, at the time of its success, normal sensibilities did not find the book morally offensive or see a bad example in its more explicit scenes. Bataillon's appeal to the literal sense of the appended moral comments (*"La Céléstine" selon Fernando de Rojas*) has, however, been contested by Lida (*Originalidad*, pp. 294–96), who lists writers who questioned its moral level, including some from the prudish eighteenth and nineteenth centuries. She mentions eight, from Vives to Gracián, who express reservations, including Lope de Vega and Cervantes. (This list is reproduced by Gilman, *The Spain*, p. 361.) However, Cervantes' comment ("... if only it revealed less of the sensual side") is mild and says nothing of how he thinks the moral efficacy (if it has any) is impaired by "lo humano," or even how little or how much of the book he thinks is overexplicit. The case of Lope de Vega (Rojas' greatest follower, in his own *La Dorotea*) is even less valid, since the stricture against *La Celestina* is voiced by a character in a play (*Juan de Dios y Antón Martín*) who is a saint in disguise! The rest, Luis Vives and five ecclesiastics, do not single out *Celestina*; they use it as a representative of all secular fiction, which, in their puritanical way, they condemn. So the matter rests where it was.[8]

## II   *Themes: Love, Death, Fortune, Conflict*[9]

We have already had occasion to make some qualitative observations on Calisto's love, by contrast with the kinds of love found most worthy by the medieval culture which he inherited. For a Christian, the only perfect love is God's and the only perfect object for man's love is God. Love for God is also the only framework within which human love can be virtuous and unselfish. This is the sense of St. Augustine's dictum that "the right will is, therefore, good love, and the wrong will is evil love" (*City of God,* bk. XIV, chap. 7). When Calisto sets

Melibea above God—he is not a Christian but "a Melibean" he says (I, 41)—Rojas shows the most fundamental aspect of that reversal of values which we commented on in chapter 7. There is no room for doubt or ambiguity here. Rojas cannot be confused with the nineteenth-century poets who exalt romantic love. Nor can Calisto's state of mind be mistaken for that love, typified in Dante's *Vita Nuova*, which is a kind of self-discipline of the emotions.

Much has been written in this century about "courtly love" in the Middle Ages, and it is usually assumed that Calisto belongs in this tradition. The phrase "courtly love" is taken to cover that idealization of love and of woman which dominates poetry and romance from the twelfth century onward, and which radiates from Provence throughout western Europe and the Mediterranean area.[10] In the broadest sense, it includes the amorous poetry of Dante, the romances of Chrétien de Troyes (where it is exposed to criticism), and the *Roman de la Rose* (where it is treated with irony), and it extends into the fifteenth century and beyond. Insofar as it is possible and allowable to generalize among so many writers, so varied in their individual styles, we may summarize the recurrent concepts of this tradition thus:

1. The superiority of the lady. She may command her admirer to do anything, and if he is a true lover, he will obey.

2. The essence of true love, then, is service. Through service the lover learns discipline and humility.

3. He protects her reputation whether she be married or single: secrecy is essential and to break secrecy is treachery, especially if he enjoys her favors.[11] Consequently, however capricious or unfeeling or cruel the lady may be, the lover must suffer in silence. Once she has admitted him into her service, he may not complain publicly in his talk or in his verses, nor may he reveal who she is.

4. By submitting himself to love, the lover does not only become a more perfect lover but a more noble man; and he becomes more "courteous" through his training in obedience, patience, and prudence.

It is clear from this summary that courtly love claims ethical values and even the cultivation of such Christian virtues as humility, fortitude, temperance, and so on. Like the Christian before God, the lover may not claim merit in the eyes of his lady but must serve until she deigns to grant him her grace. Some poets, on the other hand, paganized the relation, with prayers and offerings to Cupid or Amor or Venus. The most notable development is Dante's spiritualization of his love in the *Paradiso*, where Beatrice leads him upward to enjoy the beatific vision, where love of woman is no longer enjoyed for itself but is the agency by which he attains a more perfect love of God. There, human love is both enriched and transcended in divine love.[12] Such spiritualization is not characteristic of courtly love in general, but if it represents an exceptional elevation of the concept, Calisto represents an exceptional degradation of Dante in almost every particular (see above, chapter 6).

Courtly love was a poetic concept, and it was so varied that it is hardly accurate to call it a single tradition. From its first appearance as the *fin' amor* of Provençal poetry, it is subject to parody and irony. It tells us little about the realities of medieval life and sentiment. Perhaps such poetic conventions helped to shape noble ladies' imaginary picture of an ideal lover. Probably many aristocratic young women have *hoped* that destiny would bring them a handsome man who would be theirs alone, who would combine, as in Chrétien's notion, a proper balance of *amour* and *aventure*, doing brave things in their service and showing submissive devotion. Such hopes have corresponded to some extent to the courtship rituals of many times and places. But it would be rash to suppose that courtly-love poetry reflects a society in which women were held in peculiar veneration or given an exalted status. Certainly, the courtly fictions leave no doubt that such a form of love cannot be sustained within marriage. On the other hand, if Oscar Wilde's witticism— that life imitates art—is true, the truth of it is not found in large social patterns but in aberrant individuals or groups unaccommodated by social norms, such as all the suicides which are said to have followed the publication of Goethe's *Werther*. Calisto, his speech soaked with verbal clichés and his sentiments running unchecked among the fantasies of erotic fiction, represents in literature one of the perils of literature's feigned realities.

The inversions which characterize the structure of *La Celestina* are symbolic of a subversion of reality—intellectual and spiritual rather than simply moral—and point toward a catastrophic end. The subjection of spiritual values to those of the material world could have no other outcome than a violent reversal, a breaking of the tension in a punishment which was agreed by convention to fit the offense. This is not to say that amorous folly is always treated in the same way, but the basic oppositions are clearly expressed: "Two streams flow from the single fount of love; cupidity and charity,"[13] and medieval literature sustains this opposition, which has the authority of St. Paul (I Tim. 6:10; I Cor. 13:12). Juan de Mena, asking how can intelligent men give themselves blindly to love, likewise distinguishes between "Venus' fire" and "spotless Christian love."[14] There is idolatrous passion in Chaucer's Troilus, who, like Calisto, abandons all manly pursuits for the sake of love, prays to Cupid and Venus in pseudoreligious rapture, but also resorts to the duplicity, deceit, "covetyse" of Pandarus. He, too, inverts the natural hierarchy when he promises to be under the "yerde" (i.e., staff of authority) of Criseyde.[15] Like Calisto, he is cut off from society from the moment that he accepts the rule of passion. If the enthusiasts of courtly love enjoin the lover to secrecy so as to protect the lady's good name, here is the same situation stripped of glamour: it is not honor but shame which prevents Troilus and Calisto from revealing their love. In the *Roman de la Rose* (4221–5920), the lover is opposed by Reason who interprets the will of God. In a pseudo-Aristotelian text edited by Roger Bacon we find the thematic development of *La Celestina* succinctly expressed and, moreover, in terms of a chain of cause and effect similar to that of Rojas' plot: "So the sensual impulse leads to carnal love, carnal love in turn leads to covetousness, covetousness to greed for money, greed for money leads to loss of shame, loss of shame to insolence, and insolence to infidelity."[16] Medieval moral arguments frequently proceed in this way because the soul is thought of as organized around the faculties of will, understanding, and memory: a yielding of the will to this impulse can expose it to the next, and a laxness of the understanding here leads to a failure of perception there. Thus, we see that "sin" did not refer only, or even primarily, to the body. Sin is more seriously an affair of the mind, of failure to use the knowledge that one has (as in being too lazy or self-indulgent to profit from knowledge or experience), or sin can consist in prevarication with evil. So, we find in Thomas Aquinas the following statements: "Sins of the spirit are more culpable than sins of the flesh"; "The consummation of sin is in the consent of reason" (*Summa Theologica*, I–II, q.73, a.5; II–II, q.35, a.3). Readers may be surprised to observe that love and sin go so often together and, at the same time, that medieval writing was frequently less prudish, more frank, and yet less sensational than much modern literature. But sin, as we said, is of the mind, as literature is of the head. All sins can ultimately be classified as aspects of the one sin of disobedience, and love literature is characteristically concerned more with loyalties than with sex. Celestina indirectly confirms this observation when she says, "as for that, the donkeys in the field are better at it" (act I; I, 108).

If war (and its sporting substitutes) have been the typical field of action in literature, wherein the protagonist can reveal both his personal vigor and intelligence and his ability to represent the honor of his society, love has been the activity of the mind in which the protagonist revealed both his personal sensibility and his ability to sustain the hierarchy of values. These two great narrative themes of medieval literature are therefore complementary, because the inner man must be completed by the outer. Epic and heroic chronicle—War—take place in the open and tend to become an allegory of law and justice. Law and justice are the love bonds of a whole society. Romance and sentimental encounter—Love—take place in castles or enclosed gardens and tend to become psychomachia, conflicts in the mind between reason, the virtues, and their enemies. Reason and virtue are the law and justice of the individual and have the power to mediate the soul's harmony in an harmoniously ordered universe. A protagonist who is enslaved by passionate love could no more be presented as the hero of medieval romance than could a man who runs away in battle. This is another reason why Rojas had to call his play a comedy. Many stories of romantic love are clearly unheroic, at a period in history when no one yet had the perverse idea of exalting an antihero into a hero. Troilus turns his back upon the war and then, after losing Criseyde, becomes suicidally reckless. While loving her he loses his courage and his taste for the manly pursuit: in fact he is so unmanned by his passion that when they are finally joined, Pandarus has to lift him weeping onto her bed! Calisto was never a warrior, and it is obvious that the milieu of the play defines him not only as unheroic but antiheroic. He appears to be completely urban and not to have been apprenticed in war, as the traditional nobility were. His military accoutrements are reduced to one captive symbolic or heraldic creature, the falcon—whose first act is to get lost in Melibea's garden. From then on, the surroundings of the action are, as we have noted before, indoors or in an enclosed garden, in darkness.

We noted elsewhere (chapters 4 and 6) that Rojas puts beyond doubt Melibea's betrayal of trust, her tearing of the tissue of loyalties, which stretches beyond her into the fabric of society. Her suicide is the artistic symbol and consummation of her willful separation from the social web. As medieval philosophy saw all substance as the conjoining by love of matter and form, so in the existence of the individual the anarchic natural instincts must be shaped and completed by the forms provided in family and society. Matter is common to all, but forms create individuals. To abandon the formal component is to disintegrate the person and destroy oneself. Gilman, however (*The Art,* p. 205), stresses the tenderness and lyricism of act XIX (Melibea in her garden, see chapter 5 above). In reply, we could stress the significance of individual features of the garden, for example, the cypresses which are symbols of mourning and death, the moon—emblem of change—together with those other images of the virginity (belt, tower, walled garden) which Melibea has given away. *La Celestina* would not be the first work of literature to combine in its descriptive images a haunting lyric beauty with a firm symbolic structure, an enticement of the sensual imagination with a counterflow of evaluative signs. That is true also of a great part of the *Roman de la Rose.* However, at this point I want not merely to concede the lyric intensity of act XIX but to mark it for special attention. Once again we must not confuse such scenes with the sweet romanticism of a Lamartine or a Chateaubriand. Rather, an appropriate comparison would be with Dante.

In the episode of Paolo and Francesca (one of the best-known passages of the *Divine Comedy*) we find another love story in which literature has acted upon the imagination so that, in Dante's concise image, the book is the go-between. Francesca da Rimini, as Dante meets her after her death, is still so possessed by love that it has not weakened. Dante bows his head and weeps with grief and pity as she speaks of past torments, when she tells how she and Paolo first kissed. They were reading the romance of Lancelot together, their feelings were kindled by what they read, they exchanged glances, then drew together, "and then that day we read no farther." Dante is so overcome with emotion that he swoons with pity and falls to the ground (*Inferno* V, 91–142). Dante allows Francesca to tell her story of adulterous love with such sad eloquence and, as he listens, his own senses are wounded with such poignant sympathy that we can easily perceive how passionate love has been given the opportunity to plead its cause. And if Dante swoons, who could remain unmoved? Yet the modern reader is likely to be shocked as he reminds himself that Francesca is in hell. The most powerful appeal that this love (an engrossing human love) can send, however, is to the emotions (enemies of reason and virtue). In common with all the inhabitants of the *Inferno*, Francesca torments herself by reliving the passions of the past; hell's version of eternity is a time eternally suspended, in which no growth, no new knowledge is possible. As in Melibea's garden, the experience is always a repetition of the same experience, an elegiac prolongation of a joy already sensed as past, so that the transitoriness of it is as painful as the repetition.[17]

It is also in this passage where Francesca utters the famous words (lines 121–23) that there is no greater sorrow than to recall, when one is in misery, a time of happiness. These words contain in concentrated essence the whole complaint against Fortune which Celestina makes as she recalls her past, and Pleberio makes as he thinks of what he built and what is now fallen. The words of Francesca da Rimini echo those of Boethius in *The Consolation of Philosophy* (book II, prose 4): "in the

midst of adversity the worst misfortune is to have been happy."
At this, Philosophy reminds Boethius that Fortune is not the
touchstone of happiness, so she enumerates the many good
things he has, and declares that the mind creates its own
happiness or unhappiness. Can cruel Fortune still trouble people's
minds in hell? one might ask. In Dante's vision of hell Fortune
could scarcely be more at home. The traditional image of
goddess Fortuna with her wheel raising some and bringing
down those who thought they were secure is a most concise
emblem of a world of instability and uncertainty. Those who
suffer in the *Inferno* are in continual agitation; they, like Satan,
are condemned because they rejected God or loved something
more than Him or sought their own paradises of power and
greed. In rejecting Him they have lost the only center of peace
and repose, "the still center of the turning world." So Fortune
rules in the lower world of material possessions and desires;
the "sublunary" world as it was called, for below the moon's
sphere everything is subject to change and decay, while above it,
as one approaches heaven, all is regularity and intelligible order.

In his prologue Rojas refers to a dictum of Heraclitus, confirmed by Petrarch, which says that all things are engaged in
endless conflict and movement. The point is extended (I, 16–22)
by Rojas, and it turns to bathos as he reports the conflicting
desires of his friends—some urging that he enlarge the *Comedia,*
others that he leave it—and wonders about the conflicts of
judgment that the *Tragicomedia* will call forth. Although individual characters lament the operations of Fortune, and in doing
so quote directly from Petrarch,[18] *La Celestina* itself is not a
work designed merely to illustrate these operations. As we
have seen, all the deaths in the play are rigorously planned to
follow a sequence of cause and effect. A fussy reader, of course,
can object that missing a foothold on a ladder is not *caused*
by Calisto's seduction of Melibea; however, what has already
been said about Calisto's loss of reality, misjudgment of his
servants, and so on provides the kind of analogical connection
which satisfies artistic logic.[19] Pármeno, the only objective character at this stage, observes about Calisto's adoration of Celestina,
"He's down on the ground worshipping the most ancient and
whorish piece of dirt who was ever flogged around the brothels.

in that play we are given a tragedy of greed, and fate is personified in the Weird Sisters. That which appears to be fortune in *Celestina* is neither comically exploited nor stoically borne; it is, quite simply, the consequences of actions taken in a morally intelligible world. Acts continually lead to their consequences—which is the evidence the dramatist gives us that his fictional world is intelligible. Unlike real life, where consequences may be remote or delayed or hidden from view altogether, in drama of the classical Western tradition consequences are visible "in this life." As Oscar Wilde's Miss Prism observed with comical exactitude, "The good ended happily, and the bad unhappily. That is what Fiction means." A man like Macbeth, who plots against others, eventually has his plans turn against him. There the plot easily displays his responsibility for his own destruction. That is the kind of dramatic plot which is worked out with Sempronio, Pármeno, and Celestina. Calisto is different; he is a man who weaves no political strategems in which to become entangled but one whose offense is against nature and himself. For his case, there were no other dramatic mechanisms available to Rojas than the fall (a morally loaded image) preceded by an abundance of signposts. What else was Rojas to do? Have the hand of God blast him off the ladder with a thunderbolt? Let him live, and have old Pleberio set his fierce servants on him? Then the critic who says that Calisto's accidental fall from the ladder has only accidental significance could say (with better reason) that he was punished for being found out or because someone made a noise or betrayed him, etc. Moreover, such a solution would either elevate Calisto or (if Rojas could somehow divert the drift of sentiment toward him) give greater dramatic strength and moral significance to Pleberio. It seems obvious to me that Rojas wished to do neither of these things. (For a witty and lucid discussion of accident in drama, the penultimate chapter of Bernard Shaw's *The Quintessence of Ibsenism*, "The Technical Novelty," deserves rereading.)

Irony is a kind of double vision, by means of which discrepancies (like that between Celestina's intention in corrupting Pármeno and its consequence for her) are opened, created, and illuminated. The falls of Calisto and Melibea on the contrary (and the point was implied by George Steiner) are not ironic, because image and action coincide; the relation of sign and signified is a confirmatory one. There is irony in *El burlador de Sevilla* when Tisbea, who begins the scene fishing and haughtily despising "the foolish little fishes" and the village men in the same breath, is "hooked" by the big fish, Don Juan Tenorio who pops up from the sea. But in *King Oedipus* there is no irony when the hero physically blinds himself at the moment of discovering his figurative "blindness." As to the agency of the catastrophe, Calisto is no more killed by gravity and "alien space" than Hamlet is killed by sharpness and alien matter. Gravity is universal; for local effects we must look for local causes. Space is not alien in *Celestina,* but the very familiar medium in which this action, like any other, takes place. And the action is what matters. As E. H. Gombrich has observed, with reference to visual art: "After the many weighty tomes that have been written on how space is rendered in art, Steinberg's trick drawings serve as a welcome reminder that it is never space which is represented but familiar things in situations."[25]

### III  *Pleberio: His Master's Voice?*

The final act of *La Celestina* is almost entirely taken up with the peroration of Pleberio, the person who has had least to say until now. Every reader is bound to feel that this sudden shift in attention is full of significance; but there has been no general agreement on what the significance is. The content of his lament is, briefly, that it is unnatural for the old to be left mourning for the young; that all he has made (ships, towers, gardens) was for Melibea; that the three forces of Fortune, Love, and World (which had been constantly assailed by moralists and courted by some poets) deceive men with promises in order then to betray them. He thought he had escaped the toils of love when he married; love, which has a beautiful name, is enemy of all reason and order. The world is the trap in which men, by reason of being born, are fated for misery.

This speech is usually interpreted from one of two viewpoints: either Pleberio speaks for no one but himself or his is the voice of Rojas. There are differences within these viewpoints. For Bataillon, Pleberio is ridiculous, because he blames abstractions (Love, World, Fortune) for what has happened instead of placing blame where it belongs.[26] O. H. Green sees him as a foolish and worldly man who fails to take the Christian attitude to disaster.[27] In the view of Miss Berndt, Pleberio is moved by his bitter experiences to ask questions which the author would be unable to answer.[28] On the other side of the divide, Mrs. Malkiel considers him as both the mouthpiece of the author through whom the final judgment on the action is given, and a father who is grief-stricken and also egotistic since he feels his daughter's death as the dénouement of his own life.[29] Bruce Wardropper puts the speech formally into the history of the elegy and agrees that it expresses self-pity and also the "anguish of a man both in spite of and beyond the consolations of religion." "In grief a man is a man before he is a Christian."[30] Charles F. Fraker goes beyond this expression of natural doubt in a situation of excruciating grief to a general pessimism attributable to Rojas.[31] Frank Casa, though using as evidence the pagan elements of dramatic traditions, also asserts that Rojas confronts the "transcendental problems" of man in a universe of overwhelming forces.[32] Gilman (*The Spain of Fernando de Rojas*) finds the words of Pleberio "unorthodox in every sense" (p. 374).

The diversity of interpretations represents the range of meanings which scholars have derived from the work as a whole. In performing this act of interpretation, if we attend to both the personal expressions and the generalizations of the speaker, his past performance and his present stance, we shall note some disturbing phrases. For example: "I shall no longer have the fears and anxieties that terrified me every day; your death alone sets me free from suspicion" (II, 208). From these words one must reluctantly conclude that Pleberio now feels some relief from the jealous fears he has suffered every day for his daughter's honor. But since we saw how little communication he or his wife had with their daughter, and since even at this moment he can talk about being relieved of those anxieties, I am not persuaded that his present perplexities are the reliable vehicle for Rojas' judgment of his world. No doubt, he can tell us a great deal about desolation and about the cruelty of children: "why didn't you have pity on your dear beloved mother? Why were you so cruel to your old father?" (II, 212). But again, it can occur to him, as his daughter's corpse lies at his feet, that all his wealth and his conspicuous luxury are wasted for lack of an heir (II, 292). So it is not so clear that he can instruct us in philosophy. Charles Fraker truly says that his attack on love is "nothing less than an indictment of the very idea of the goodness of nature" (art. cit., p. 523). But this must be seen within the larger moral vision: "Concupiscence is vulnerability. The very things the concupiscent person has set his heart on are so many gaps in the defense against Fortune's onslaught. The less the moral integrity, the more one is apt to be caught up in the net of circumstance" (p. 525). Fraker is here putting into perspective the drama of Calisto; it surely applies equally to Pleberio. Pleberio confesses to having sowed his own wild oats until he turned forty and settled down (II, 208); he himself seems to suggest that he is a Calisto who got away with it, in keeping with his character as a calculator: "I didn't know you [Love] avenged yourself on the children for what their fathers do" (II, 209). In brief, the old, who are conventionally assumed to have learned wisdom and detachment are, after all, as foolish and as passionately attached to their lives as the young are. If Calisto lacks heroic vigor, the characteristic virtue of the young man in literature, Pleberio lacks wisdom and dignity, the exemplary qualities of the old. Such a view, I suggest, neither coats the play with moralism nor does it detract from Rojas' pessimism, which is part of his moral *vision*, inherent in the whole play and not limited to any single role. T. S. Eliot wrote in *Burnt Norton*, "Human kind / cannot bear very much reality," words which could well serve as an epigraph for *La Celestina*. Perhaps they might also explain why it is that critics still tirelessly search the play for a residual hero, even at the risk of allegory. A generation ago, it was a Renaissance "love of life" supposedly embodied in the lovers and in Celestina; now it is the "cosmic pessimism" of Pleberio.

In this short space it is impossible to do justice to the varied and subtle arguments which this final speech has provoked, so

I refrain from pressing to a conclusion. It is worth noting, however, since none of the commentators does so, that Pleberio's (and the book's) last words, "why did you leave me wretched and alone *in hac lacrymarum valle?*" allude to the hymn *Salve regina*.[33] That is a hymn which assumes nothing less than that we are all Pleberios in our misfortunes but also that we are *aware* of our insufficiency and our unwisdom: "we call upon you . . . wailing and weeping; we sigh to you in this vale of tears (*in hac lacrymarum valle*)." The hymn, sung from the depth of human agony, prays for help and still shouts a hopeful *Salve!* to Mary, and a blessing on Jesus. It reminds us (while Pleberio seemingly forgets his wife lying at his feet in a swoon) that grief finds hope and consecration in sharing the suffering of others. "The world" is indeed frightening and full of evil, as poet after poet tells us throughout the Middle Ages, but there is no other place in which to win salvation, and no one promised that it would be easy. Poor confused Pleberio, lacking the advantages of the spectator, gropes in the dark night of his grief for an explanation. At the last hour of the day—and every day—as the lights were extinguished in churches and monasteries all over Christendom, the *Salve regina* was sung at the end of the office of Compline. *In hac lacrymarum valle* were the last words of the Church, in which it recognized the universality of pain and sorrow, symbolically put out the candles, and waited for the new day.

## IV   *The Social Dimension*

The fact that Rojas was a converso has led some critics to suppose that Jewish blood was what prevented Calisto from asking for Melibea's hand in marriage. This fact has also been made to account for Rojas' assumed religious skepticism. However, Proust made a valuable observation (in *Contre Sainte-Beuve*) when he wrote that "a book is the product of a different 'I' from that which we display in our habits, in society, and in our vices,"[34] and Gilman is surely on firm ground when he says that we need not imagine Rojas "always walking in fear and trembling, beset constantly by hordes of self-appointed spies for the Holy Office" (*The Spain*, p. 478), nor must we look for secret messages in *La Celestina* (p. 366). And his positive thesis in this book—that there is in *La Celestina* a special, unique irony or distance between the play and the commonplace moral formulas of the time, which derives from the marginal situation of being a converso—is argued with sustained brilliance. Not that it can ever be proved: there is equal cogency in the remark by T. E. May, "His work owes a good deal of its impact to its combination of a youthful trenchancy of moral idealism with disillusion about life as it is generally lived."[35]

Juan Antonio Maravall, in *El mundo social de "La Celestina,"* develops the thesis that the play represents the crisis in Spain at the transition from a feudal, patriarchal, and austere rural aristocracy, whose economic base is land and whose values are honor and service, to a bourgeois, ostentatious, and urban nobility, devoted to display and consumption, based on trade and finance, and whose value is wealth. In such a transition, personal loyalties are being dissolved by mercenary relationships, money enables servants to be hired instead of being raised in the family, and all values are expressible in monetary terms. This is why Rojas, conservative in outlook, projects his pessimistic view through the image of a world of prostitution.

Finally, whether we consider the pessimism of Pleberio or the pessimism of a "social reality" to be the final lingering chord of *La Celestina*, we should not miss the clear bright note of Sosia. He is the one character who grows, trusts, is fooled, listens, and learns something about himself—and therefore about "the world"—in his brief appearance. He, with his sharp simplicity, balances the gaudy strumpet Areusa as she spreads out to fill the vacant plot left by Celestina. If the comparison could avoid misleading by its suggestion of heroic grandeur, one might say that he is to *La Celestina* what young Fortinbras is to *Hamlet*.

# Notes and References

## Chapter One

1. The most complete and the most enlightening account of Rojas' biography, his family, and the social consequences of converso status, is given in Stephen Gilman, *The Spain of Fernando de Rojas* (Princeton: Princeton University Press, 1973) (hereafter cited as *The Spain*).

2. F. del Valle Lersundi, "Documentos referentes a Fernando de Rojas," *Revista de Filología Española* 12 (1925), 391 (hereafter cited as "Documentos").

3. Manuel Serrano y Sanz, "Noticias biográficas de Fernando de Rojas autor de *La Celestina* . . . , *Revista de Archivos, Bibliotecas y Museos* 6 (1902), 252 (hereafter cited as "Noticias").

4. Rojas' father-in-law himself testified in 1525 that his daughter was aged thirty-five (Serrano y Sanz, "Noticias," p. 263.). In another deposition in the year 1571, the ages of the Rojas' children confirm the likelihood that the marriage took place in 1507 or shortly thereafter (Gilman, *The Spain*, p. 210).

5. Gilman, *The Spain*, p. 207, n. 3, citing the personal archives of the late Don Fernando del Valle Lersundi, a descendant of Rojas.

6. Serrano y Sanz, "Noticias," p. 269.

7. Quoted by Serrano y Sanz, "Noticias," p. 246.

8. Fernando del Valle Lersundi, "Testamento de Fernando de Rojas, autor de *La Celestina*," *Revista de Filología Española* 16 (1929), 366–88. The will is reproduced on pages 366–70 (hereafter cited as "Testamento").

9. The inventory is published in "Testamento," pp. 371–88.

10. The site is described by Luis Careaga, "Investigaciones referentes a Fernando de Rojas," *Revista Hispánica Moderna* 4 (1937–38), 193–208.

11. "Testamento," p. 379.

12. The Scottish universities still retain the division into "nations," for certain purposes.

13. For a fuller account, see E. Esperabé Arteaga, *Historia pragmática e interna de la Universidad de Salamanca* (Salamanca: Nuñez Izquierdo, 1914); V. de la Fuente, *Historia de las Universidades,*

*colegios y demás centros de enseñanza* (Madrid: Viuda e Hija de Fuentenebro, 1884–89); Aubrey F. G. Bell, *Luis de León* (Oxford: Oxford University Press, 1925); Gilman, *The Spain,* chap. 6.

14. The earliest records indicate 1473 as the first year of printing in both Barcelona and Valencia; see F. J. Norton, *Printing in Spain, 1501–1520* (Cambridge: Cambridge University Press, England, 1966), pp. 78, 94.

15. Gilman, *The Spain,* pp. 310–34; R. Menéndez Pidal, "La Lengua en tiempos de los Reyes Católicos," *Cuadernos Hispano-Americanos* 13 (1950), 9–24.

16. The throne of St. Peter was occupied in succession, by Innocent VIII (1484–92), who officiated at the political marriage of his own bastard son to a daughter of the Medici, in the Vatican palace; Alexander VI (1492–1503), better known as Rodrigo Borgia, who in 1494 made a military alliance with the Turks against France; Julius II (1503–13), who made and betrayed alliances and led his soldiers into battle; Leo X (1513–21), whose first words after his election (it is reported) were, "God has given us the Papacy: now we'll make the most of it!"

17. See Juan Antonio Maravall, *El mundo social de "La Celestina"* (Madrid: Gredos, 1964).

18. This *Oration* may be read in English in *The Renaissance Philosophy of Man,* edited by Ernst Cassirer, Paul Oskar Kristeller, and John H. Randall, Jr. (Chicago: University of Chicago Press, 1948) and separately in the translation by A. R. Caponigri (Chicago: Henry Regnery Co., 1954).

19. See Marie Boas, *The Scientific Renaissance (1450–1630)* (New York: Harper and Row, 1966), chaps. 3, 5.

20. See Gilman, *The Spain,* Appendix 3.

21. F. del Valle Lersundi, "Documentos."

22. "Noticias biográficas," p. 249.

23. Gilman, *The Spain,* p. 45.

24. *Ibid.,* p. 31.

25. Gilman is convinced of the falsification, and his argument is persuasive, *The Spain,* pp. 26–50.

26. Gilman, *The Spain,* pp. 49–50.

27. The reader will find these matters argued at length in the works of the late Américo Castro, notably in *La realidad histórica de España* (Mexico: Porrúa, 1962); *De la edad conflictiva,* 2nd ed. enlarged (Madrid, 1963); *La Celestina como contienda literaria* (Madrid: Revista de Occidente, 1965). Also of importance are Albert A. Sicroff, *Les controverses des statuts de pureté de sang en*

*Espagne du XVᵉ au XVIIᵉ siècle* (Paris: Didier, 1960); A. Domín-
guez Ortiz, *La clase social de los conversos en Castilla en la edad
moderna* (Madrid: Consejo Superior de Investigaciones Cientificas,
n.d.); Nicolás López Martínez, *Los judaizantes castellanos y la
Inquisición en tiempo de Isabel la Catolica* (Burgos: Seminario Met-
ropolitano de Burgos, 1954); Cecil Roth, *A History of the Marranos*
(Philadelphia: Jewish Publ. Soc. of America, 1932); Yitzhak F. Baer,
*A History of the Jews in Christian Spain* (Philadelphia: Jewish Publ.
Soc. of America, 1966); Gilman, *The Spain.*

28. The former kingdoms of Aragon, Catalonia, and Valencia were
more relaxed, pluralistic societies than Castile, and had long sustained mercantile and political relations with Italy and the Mediterranean.

29. *Casta* is the word used by Américo Castro to denote each of
the three segments (Christians, Moors, Jews) which made up the
society of medieval Spain in long periods of tranquility until the
late fourteenth century, and which later included the "Old Christians" and conversos. The word implies racial identity through its
use by animal breeders to mean "stock" or "breed." The adjective
*castizo* means "purebred"; applied to language, artifacts, etc. it means
"pure," "in a pure traditional style," "untainted" by foreign influ-
ences. For Castro, it was important to recognize that the caste arises
within the society by one part projecting its sense of separateness
on another part. The tragedy of the situation we are describing is
not that the conversos wanted to be different, but the very opposite—they wanted to be integrated. So did the Jews before they were
expelled, and many of the Sephardim have kept their Spanish speech,
Spanish songs, Spanish proverbs, and Spanish traditional lore to this
day wherever they settled—the Balkans, Turkey, Tunis, etc. Castro
was careful to stress the overriding Spanishness of these "castes" by
the use of compound epithets: *hispanocristiano, hispanomorisco, his-
panojudaico* ("Hispano-Christian," "Hispano-Moorish," "Hispano-
Judaic").

30. Cited in Gilman, *The Spain*, p. 161.

31. M. Serrano y Sanz, "Noticias," p. 262.

32. Gilman, *The Spain*, pp. 39–42. The quotation is from pp. 41–42.

33. Dr. Lorenzo Galíndez de Carvajal wrote a report on the
Emperor Charles the Fifth's Royal Council. The criterion by which
each member was judged was not his competence or integrity, but
"cleanness of blood." The writer recommends that only men of peasant background be appointed (cited in Américo Castro, *De la edad
conflictiva*, p. 197).

## Chapter Two

1. Most recently by J. Homer Herriott, *Toward a Critical Edition of the "Celestina"* (Madison: University Press of Wisconsin, 1964).

2. See Stephen Gilman, *The Art of "La Celestina"* (Madison, 1956), Appendix B (hereafter cited as *The Art*).

3. F. J. Norton, *Printing in Spain, 1501–1520* Appendix B, "The Early Editions of the *Celestina*."

4. Sir Henry Thomas, "Antonio [Martínez] de Salamanca, printer of *La Celestina*, Rome, c. 1525," *The Library*, 5th ser. 8 (1953), 45–50; Norton, *Printing*, pp. 153–54.

5. Norton, *Printing*, p. 155.

6. Herriott (*Toward a Critical Edition*) lists more than ten thousand variants.

7. Not all were published in Spain: Spanish books were printed in the Low Countries and also in Italy.

8. "Libro, en mi opinión, divi— / Si encubriera más lo huma—."

9. Quoted by M. Menéndez Pelayo, *Orígenes de la novela*, III, *Edición Nacional de las obras completas de M. P.*, vol. XV (Santander, 1943), p. 390 (hereafter cited as *Orígenes*, III).

10. For example, Daniel Poyán, editing a facsimile of the Toledo 1500 *Comedia* (Zurich: Bibliotheca Bodmeriana, 1961), and José Montero Padilla in *Arbor* 54 (1963), argue that the Toledo, 1500 text is earlier than the Burgos, 1499.

11. Edited by G. D. Trotter and K. Whinnom (London: Tamesis Books, 1969).

12. M. Menéndez Pelayo, *Orígenes* IV, 3–198; Gilman, *The Spain*, pp. 362–63 give interesting discussions of these works.

13. See R. O. Jones, *The Golden Age: Prose and Poetry, A Literary History of Spain*, vol. II. (London: Benn, and New York: Barnes and Noble, 1971), pp. 64–65.

14. Edited by Edwin S. Morby, 2nd edition (Berkeley, University of California Press, 1968).

## Chapter Three

1. Juan de Valdés, *Diálogo de la lengua*, ed. J. F. Montesinos (Madrid: Clásicos castellanos, 1964), p. 182.

2. Marcelino Menéndez Pelayo, *Orígenes* III, p. 257.

3. C. A. Eggert, "Zur Frage der Urheberschaft der Celestina," *Zeitschrift für Romanische Philologie* 21 (1897), 32–42.

4. *Orígenes* III, p. 259.

5. Stephen Gilman, *The Art*, p. 9.

6. Proaza has been exonerated of any unusual interference in the publication of the book by D. W. McPheeters, "Alonso de Proaza and the *Celestina*," *Hispanic Review* 24 (1956), 13–25; *idem. El humanista español Alonso de Proaza* (Valencia: Castalia, 1961).

7. R. Foulché-Delbosc, "Observations sur *La Célestine*," *Revue Hispanique* 7 (1900), 28–80; *idem.*, 9 (1902), 171–99.

8. In chronological order: Ralph E. House, Margaret Mulroney, and Ilse G. Probst, "Notes on the Authorship of the *Celestina*," *Philological Quarterly* 3 (1924), 81–91; J. Vallejo, F. Castro Guisasola, and M. Herrero García, "Notas sobre *La Celestina*: ¿Uno o dos autores?" *Revista de Filología Española* 11 (1924), 402–12; Ruth Davis, "New Data on the Authorship of Act I of the *Comedia de Calisto y Melibea*," *University of Iowa Studies in Spanish Language and Literature* (Iowa City, 1928); José V. Montesino Samperio, "Sobre la cuantificación del estilo literario: Una contribución al estudio de la unidad de autor en *La Celestina* de Fernando de Rojas," *Revista Nacional de Cultura* 55 (1946), 94–115; 56 (1946), 63–68; Giulia Adinolfi, "*La Celestina* e la sua unità di composizione," *Filologia Romanza* 1 (1954), 12–60; M. Criado de Val, *Indice verbal de "La Celestina"* (Madrid, 1955).

9. The debate continues; witness the interesting observations of Francisco Ruiz Ramón, "Nota sobre la autoría del Acto I de *La Celestina*," *Hispanic Review* 42 (1974), 431–35.

## Chapter Five

1. There is a published version, by Luis Escobar and Huberto Pérez de la Ossa (Madrid, 1959), which was performed in Paris at the Palais des Nations, in April, 1958.

2. Ferdinand Wolf, *Studien zur Geschichte der Spanischen und Portugiesischen Nationalliteratur* (Berlin: Asher, 1859); the relevant parts of this work are translated and reprinted in "Sobre el drama español—*La Celestina* y sus traducciones," *La España Moderna* 7, no. 80 (1895), 99–123.

3. The German text is given in a footnote in Menéndez Pelayo, *Orígenes*, III, p. 222.

4. *Orígenes*, III, p. 220. The original edition of this work appeared in 1907 and repeats the basic position which the author took in his edition of *La Celestina* (Vigo, 1899–1900).

5. "procura, no imitar, sino ensanchar y superar, aprovechando sus elementos y fundiéndolos en una concepción nueva del amor, de la vida y del arte." *Orígenes*, III, p. 221.

6. *Orígenes*, III, p. 223.

7. "El título de *novela dramática* que algunos han querido dar a la obra del bachiller Rojas, nos parece inexacto y contradictorio en los términos. Si es drama, no es novela. Si es novela, no es drama. El fondo de la novela y del drama es uno mismo, la representación estética de la vida humana; pero la novela la representa en forma de *narración*, el drama en forma de *acción*. Y todo es activo, y nada es narrativo en la *Celestina, ..."* *ibid.*, p. 222.

8. In his short story *Las fortunas de Diana;* Lida, *La originalidad artística de "La Celestina,"* (Buenos Aires, 1961), p. 56 (hereafter cited as *Originalidad*).

9. Lida, *Originalidad*, p. 58.

10. George Steiner, *The Death of Tragedy*, (New York: Hill and Wang, 1961), p. 248.

11. Edwin J. Webber, *"The Celestina* as an *arte de amores,"* *Modern Philology* 55 (1958), 145–53.

12. Marcel Bataillon, *"La Célestine"* *selon Fernando de Rojas* (Paris: Didier, 1961), ch. III.

13. This concept was first formulated, under the name of "psychical distance," by Edward Bullough, " 'Psychical Distance' as a Factor in Art and in Aesthetic Principle," *British Journal of Psychology* 5 (1912). It is conveniently discussed in John Hospers, *Meaning and Truth in the Arts* (Chapel Hill: The University of North Carolina Press, 1946), pp. 4–9.

14. E.g., as noted by Bataillon, *La Célestine*, pp. 85–92; Lida, *La originalidad*, chap. 5.

15. For a discussion of the relation between genre and author as it has been expounded by theorists, see Paul Hernadi, *Beyond Genre* (Ithaca, N.Y., Cornell University Press, 1972), chapter 2. In addition to Hernadi's book, guidance in genre studies can be found in René Wellek and Austin Warren, *Theory of Literature*, rev. ed. (New York: Harcourt, Brace, 1966).

16. Quoted by Boris Eichenbaum, "The Theory of the Formal Method" in *Russian Formalist Criticism: Four Essays*, trans. Lee T. Lemon and Marion J. Reis (Lincoln, Nebr.: University of Nebraska Press, 1965), p. 134.

17. Ernst Robert Curtius, *European Literature and the Latin Middle Ages* (New York: Pantheon Books, 1953). Reprint (New York: Harper and Row, 1963), pp. 436–43.

18. Compare the definitions given by Dante in his letter to Can Grande della Scala.

19. Texts in Edélestand du Méril, *Poésies inédites du moyen âge* (Paris: Franck, 1854); Gustave Cohen, *La 'comédie' latine en*

*France au XIIᵉ siècle* (Paris: Sociéte d'édition "Les Belles Lettres," 1931).

20. Lida, *Originalidad*, chapter 1; Justo García Soriano, *El teatro universitario y humanístico en España* (Toledo: Gómez, 1945). Ten Latin plays have recently been edited with Italian translations in Vito Pandolfi and Erminia Artese, *Teatro goliardico dell' Umanesimo* (Milano, Lerici, 1965).

21. In his edition of Johannes de Vallata, *Poliodorus* (Madrid: Consejo Superior de Investigaciones Científicas, 1953), J. M. Casas Homs lists (pp. 70f) some youthful authors (in cases where age is known): Johannes himself (aged 18); Vergerio wrote *Paulus*, probably in 1390, aged 20; Leonardo Bruni wrote *Poliscena* between 1390–95, aged 21–26; Leone Battista Alberti was 20 when he wrote *Philodoxus*; and Gregorio Corrario composed *Procne* at age 18.

22. Edited by E. Lovarini (Bologna, 1928); Lida, *La originalidad*, pp. 46–47.

23. This speech follows the following pattern of rhetorical questions and exclamations: "O ...! O ...! O ...! If only ...! Why did you ...? Why did you ...? Why did you ...? O ...! Did you not ...? Did you not ...? In whom is there loyalty? Where is there truth? Who is without deceit? Where ...? Who ...? Who ...? Where ...? Who ...?" (II, 83–84).

24. Allardyce Nicol, *Development of the Theatre* (London: Harrap, 1927); *idem.*, *Masks, Mimes and Miracles* (New York: Cooper Square, 1963); E. K. Chambers, *The Medieval Stage* (Oxford: Oxford University Press, 1903); Silvio d'Amico, *Storia della letteratura drammatica* (Milano: Garzanti, 1950), vol. I.

25. *Poetics*, 48a 19.

26. I borrow this optical metaphor from Susanne K. Langer, *Feeling and Form* (New York: Charles Scribner's Sons, 1953).

27. For Gilman, on space as cause, see *The Art*, pp. 128, 135.

28. *Poetics*, 52a 22, "... a change to the opposite of actions performed according to probability or necessity."

29. An interesting study of such recollections is given by Dorothy Severin, *Memory in "La Celestina"* (London: Támesis Books, 1970). Unfortunately the author overlooks the obvious fact that memory has a vital part in the structure of every tragedy or black comedy from *Oedipus* and *Prometheus Bound* to *Waiting for Godot*, and beyond. The "present" time of tragedy looks both ways.

### Chapter Six

1. *Originalidad*, pp. 283–84.
2. *"La Célestine" selon Fernando de Rojas.*

3. *The Art,* chapter 3, "The Art of Character."

4. Gilman's *The Art* contains numerous euphemistic expressions of this kind. Thus, it is my guess that "trajectories of lives" (p. 74, etc.) replaces the four-letter word "plot" (a word which also disgusted Bernard Shaw).

5. A sentence like the following, "Thus, while we may not have 'characters' in *La Celestina,* Rojas knows well how to manage the characterizations furnished by the dialogue" (p. 67), creates an ideal sequence in which the utterance precedes both the speaker and the author.

6. The term "motif" was given precise formulation by folklorists Stith Thompson, Antti Arne, Vladimir Propp, and it was enlarged in literary application by the Russian Formalists in the 1920s. So Boris Tomashevsky writes, "The usual device for grouping and string-ing together motifs is the creation of a character who is the living embodiment of a given collection of motifs. . . . The character is a guiding thread which makes it possible to untangle a conglomeration of motifs and permits them to be classified and arranged." *Russian Formalist Criticism,* pp. 87–88.

7. Sources and antecedents are abundantly documented and meticulously examined in Lida, *Originalidad.*

8. E.g., in act XIV, "Go in quietly, so they won't hear you in the house" (II, 122).

9. J. A. Maravall, *El mundo social de "La Celestina."*

10. "La nota básica del carácter de Calisto es su egoísmo" (*Originalidad,* p. 347).

11. *Ibid.,* p. 351.

12. *Ibid.,* p. 350.

13. "Pero la inadaptación a la realidad, con su alternativa entre exaltación y depresión, son sí notas típicas de la adolescencia que, significativamente, Calisto ha retenido fuera de su término común," *Ibid.,* p. 354. Compare the excellent chapter, "Le Caliste insensé" in Bataillon (chap. 6, note 1).

14. Ovid, *Amores,* II, 4; Juan Ruiz, *Libro de buen amor,* stanzas 156–58.

15. Calderón's plays of wife murder, *A secreto agravio, secreta venganza* (Secret Offense, Secret Vengeance) and *El médico de su honra* (The Surgeon of His Honor), and, in modern times, Lorca's plays of family tension, *La Zapatera prodigiosa* (The Amazing Shoe-maker's Wife) and *La casa de Bernarda Alba* (The House of Ber-narda Alba), may not be accurate reflections of life, but they do reflect real anxieties which underlay conformity and ostracism.

16. O. H. Green, "La furia de Melibea," *Clavileño* 4, 20 (1953), 1–3; A. D. Deyermond "The Text-book Mishandled: Andreas Capellanus and the Opening Scene of *La Celestina*," *Neophilologus* 45 (1961), 218–21; J. M. Aguirre, *Calisto y Melibea, amantes cortesanos* (Zaragoza: Colección Almenara, 1962).

17. See chapter 5, n. 19.

18. There are two good recent translations of this poem: one by R. Mignani and M. di Cesare (Albany: The State University of New York Press, 1970) and the other in the bilingual edition by R. S. Willis (Princeton: Princeton University Press, 1972).

19. The most thorough and perceptive comparison of Celestina with preceding examples of the type is to be found in Lida de Malkiel, *Originalidad*, pp. 534–72. Also useful are A. Bonilla y San Martín, "Antecedentes del tipo celestinesco en la literatura latina," *Revue Hispanique* 15 (1906), 372–86; F. Castro Guisasola, *Observaciones sobre las fuentes literarias de La Celestina* (Madrid: *Revista de Filología Española*, Anejo V, 1924).

20. A fundamental text on *cupiditas* ("cupidity," or "greed") is St. Augustine, *De doctrina christiana* (*On Christian Doctrine*), III, x, 16.

21. It has already been remarked that Pármeno's sarcastic praise of her to Calisto (act I: see commentary) is a parody of the great canticle *Benedicite, omnia opera*.

22. *Originalidad*, pp. 265–80.

### Chapter Seven

1. This is a slogan which could only exist in an age of slogans and "ad-men" like our own. Consider the statement "X is not a cola, and it's not a root beer. It's just smooth and easy and it goes down good," where the message is: "For your information, we're not telling you what it is. It's like the grammar; you're better off not knowing."

2. Gilman, *The Spain*, p. 377.

3. I must reiterate that I am not here discussing the content of Pleberio's speech but the probability of that speech having larger significance in view of the speaker's status in the plot-structure.

4. For example that Melibea—or Calisto—was Jewish. See, for example, E. Orozco Díaz, "*La Celestina*. Hipótesis para una interpretacion," *Insula* 12, no. 124 (1957) 1, 10; F. Garrido Pallardó, *Los problemas de Calisto y Melibea, y el conflicto de su autor* (Figueras: Canigó, 1957); J. Rodríguez-Puértolas, "Nueva aproximación a *La Celestina*," *Estudios Filológicos*, No. 5 (1969) and *Anuario de Estudios Medievales* (1969), 411–32.

5. Lida, *Originalidad*, p. 217–20.

6. *Essays*, I, 19.

7. Gilman, *The Art*, p. 216.

8. The following are recent studies on this topic: E. R. Curtius, *European Literature and the Latin Middle Ages*, pp. 94–98; Giuseppe Cochiara, *Il mondo alla riversa* (Turin, 1963); Helen F. Grant, "The World Upside-Down," in *Studies in Spanish Literature of the Golden Age, presented to Edward M. Wilson*, ed. R. O. Jones (London: Támesis Books, 1973).

9. Baltasar Gracián said, "If you want to see the things of this world right, turn them upside down" ("las cosas del mundo todas se han de mirar al revés para verlas derecho"). *El criticón*, I, viii.

10. Erwin Panofsky, *Studies in Iconology* (New York: Harper and Row, 1962); George Ferguson, *Signs and Symbols in Christian Art* (Oxford: Oxford University Press, 1954); F. R. Webber, *Church Symbolism*, 2nd ed., rev. (Detroit: Gale Research Co., 1971).

11. Raymond Barbera, "Medieval Iconography in *La Celestina*," *Romanic Review* 61 (1970), 5–13; F. M. Weinberg, "Aspects of Symbolism in *La Celestina*," *Modern Language Notes* 86 (1971), 136–53.

### Chapter Eight

1. Octavio Paz, *The Bow and the Lyre* (Austin, Texas, and London: Texas University Press, 1973), p. 203. The original is *El arco y la lira*, rev. ed. (Mexico, 1967).

2. Vladimir Nabokov, "On a Book Entitled *Lolita*," in *Nabokov's Congeries*, ed. Page Stegner (New York: Viking Press 1968) p. 231.

3. "Sapientia respicit cognitionem, sicut ars operationem." Cited by Edgar de Bruyne, *The Esthetics of the Middle Ages* (New York: Ungar, 1969).

4. *Summa Theologica* Iᵃ, IIᵃᵉ, q.57, a.5: cited in de Bruyne, *Esthetics* p. 146, and in his more substantial *Études d'esthétique médiévale* (Bruges: Rijksuniversitat te Gent, 1946), III, 327.

5. Gilman, *The Art*, pp. 121–23; Lida, *Originalidad*, see analysis of each character.

6. Charles F. Fraker, Jr., "María Rosa Lida on the *Celestina*," *Hispania* 50 (1967), 178.

7. A similar interpretation can be made of the conflicting truths in the *Libro de buen amor*: see my "Verdad y verdades en el *Libro de buen amor*," *Actas del III Congreso Internacional de Hispanistas, 1968* (México: El Colegio de México, 1970), pp. 315–22.

8. In fact, we know very little about how individual works were judged in this period, apart from a few noisy controversies. Some

sidelight is shed by Miguel Herrero García, *Estimaciones literarias del siglo XVII* (Madrid: Editorial Voluntad, 1930); Otis H. Green, "La Celestina and the Inquisition," *Hispanic Review* 15 (1947), 211–16.

9. For a systematic account of these topics the following are useful: C. S. Lewis, *The Discarded Image* (Cambridge: Cambridge Universty Press, 1964; paperback ed., 1967); J. Huizinga, *The Waning of the Middle Ages* (London: Arnold, 1924); Otis H. Green, *Spain and the Western Tradition*, 4 vols. (Madison: University Press of Wisconsin, 1963–66; reprint ed., 1968); Erna Ruth Berndt, *Amor, muerte y fortuna en "La Celestina"* (Madrid: Gredos, 1963).

10. Recent contributions to the debate over courtly love include the following: Peter Dronke, *Medieval Latin and the Rise of European Love Lyric* (Oxford, 1965); Moshé Lazar, *Amour courtois et "fin' amors" dans la littérature du XIIe siècle* (Paris: Klincksieck, 1964); *The Meaning of Courtly Love*, ed. F. X. Newman (Albany: The State University of New York Press, 1968). A good brief discussion of the subject is the introduction to June Hall Martin, *Love's Fools* (London: Támesis Books, 1972).

11. The dire consequences of flouting this rule are illustrated in the anonymous French *lai* of *La Chatelaine de Vergi.* For an English version, see *Lays of Courtly Love*, verse translation by Patricia Terry (New York: Doubleday, 1963).

12. The outstanding example before Dante is the *Rima CII* of Cino da Pistoia, "Quando potrò io dir: 'Dolce mio dio. . . .' "

13. Hugo of St. Victor, in *Patrologiae cursus completus: series Latina*, ed. J. P. Migne, CLXXVI, 15.

14. *Labertino de Fortuna*, ed. John G. Cummins (Salamanca: Anaya, 1968), lines 867–72; 905–12. Many such statements can be found in Erna R. Berndt's useful *Amor, muerte y fortuna en "La Celestina."*

15. D. W. Robertson, Jr. "The Concept of Courtly Love as an Impediment to the Understanding of Medieval Texts," in F. X. Newman, ed., *The Meaning of Courtly Love*, pp. 14–15.

16. "Conatus igitur voluptatis generat carnalem amorem. Carnalis autem amor generat avariciam, avaricia generat desiderium diviciarum; desiderium diviciarum generat inverecondiam; inverecondia presumpcionem, presumcio infidelitatem," in Roger Bacon, *Opera hactenus inedita*, ed. Robert Steele, fasc. 1 (Oxford: Oxford University Press, 1905), p. 34.

17. Dante "so manages the description, he so heightens the excuse, that the excuse reveals itself as precisely the sin. . . . the persistent

parleying with the occasion of sin, the sweet prolonged laziness of love, is the first surrender of the soul to Hell. . . . the poetic sin is their shrinking from the adult love demanded of them, and their refusal of the opportunity of glory." Charles Williams, *The Figure of Beatrice* (London: Faber and Faber, 1943) p. 118. People were held to blame, not "situations."

18. A. D. Deyermond, *The Petrarchan Sources of "La Celestina"* (Oxford: Oxford University Press, 1961).

19. P. E. Russell in a review article (*Bulletin of Hispanic Studies* 41 [1964], 236) mentions the occurrence related by Peter Martyr in 1524, of the fall from a ladder and death of Francisco de Vargas, who was in the habit of visiting a noble nun "for amorous purposes." Various explanations were given; "everyone, though, was agreed in seeing the fall as proof that Heaven does not allow such deeds to go unpunished."

20. *The Death of Tragedy*, p. 13.

21. St. Augustine (see Frederick Copleston, S. J., *A History of Philosophy* (London: Burns, Oates, 1950) vol. II, *Augustine to Scotus*, p. 81); Boethius, *Consolation of Philosophy*, bk II, poem 8; Cervantes, *Persiles y Segismunda*, bk III, chap. 1.

22. Marsilio Ficino, *Epistolae*, II, 1. English trans. "Five Questions Concerning the Mind," in *The Renaissance Philosophy of Man*, ed. Ernst Cassirer, Paul Oskar Kristeller, and John Herman Randall, Jr. (Chicago, 1948), pp. 198–202. So also Cervantes in *Trabajos de Persiles y Segismunda* (The Labors of Persiles and Segismunda), III, 1: "our souls are in continual movement and cannot cease or rest except in their center which is God; for this they were created" ("nuestras almas están siempre en continuo movimiento, y no pueden parar ni sosegar sino en su centro, que es Dios, para que fueron creadas").

23. "The Fall of Fortune: From Allegory to Fiction," *Filologia Romanza* 4 (1957), 337–54.

24. Known in Lydgate's fifteenth-century English version as *The Fall of Princes*.

25. *Art and Illusion*, 2d ed. rev. (Princeton: Princeton University Press, 1961), p. 240.

26. *La Celéstine*, chap. 6.

27. "Did the World Create Pleberio?" *Romanische Forschungen* 77 (1965), 108–10.

28. *Amor, muerte y fortuna . . .* , p. 175.

29. *Originalidad*, p. 473.

30. Bruce W. Wardropper, "Pleberio's Lament for Melibea and

the Medieval Elegiac Tradition," *Modern Language Notes* 79 (1964), 140–52. Quotations are from pp. 152, 148.

31. Charles F. Fraker, Jr., "The Importance of Pleberio's Soliloquy," *Romanische Forschungen* 78 (1966), 515–29.

32. Frank Casa, "Pleberio's Lament for Melibea," *Zeitschrift für Romanische Philologie* 84 (1968), 20–29.

33. Text in *The Oxford Book of Medieval Latin Verse*, ed. F. J. E. Raby (Oxford: Oxford University Press, 1959) no. 141, p. 196.

34. "Un livre est le produit d'un autre moi que celui que nous manifestons dans nos habitudes, dans la société, dans nos vices," quoted by Serge Doubrowsky, *Pourquoi la nouvelle critique?* (Paris: Mercure de France, 1966), p. 209.

35. "The Status of Lechery," anonymous review [by T. E. May] in *The Times Literary Supplement*, Feb. 25, 1965.

# Selected Bibliography

PRIMARY SOURCES

1. Principal editions of *La Celestina*

*Comedia de Calisto y Melibea*. Burgos, 1499. There is a modern printed edition of this text edited by R. Foulché-Delbosc (Macon, Madrid, Barcelona, 1902); also a facsimile published by Archer M. Huntington (New York: De Vinne Press, 1909).

*Comedia de Calisto y Melibea*. Toledo, 1500. Facsimile edition by Daniel Poyán (Zurich, 1961).

*Comedia de Calisto y Melibea*. Sevilla, 1501. Modern printed edition by R. Foulché-Delbosc (Barcelona, 1900).

It is not known when the first *Tragicomedia* appeared; all those editions dated Sevilla 1502 are now known to have been printed much later (see chapter Two).

The best edition appears to be the following:

*Tragicomedia de Calisto y Melibea*. Valencia, 1514.

The most widely used modern editions are the following:

Fernando de Rojas. *La Celestina*. Edited by Julio Cejador y Frauca (Madrid: Espasa Calpe, 1913), 2 vols., frequently reprinted. This is a composite text based on Burgos, 1499 and Valencia, 1514 (see chapter 2).

————. *Tragicomedia de Calixto y Melibea, libro llamado también "La Celestina."* Madrid: C.S.I.C., 1958. Edited by M. Criado de Val and G. D. Trotter. This is based on one of the now discredited Sevilla, 1502 editions.

————. *La Celestina*. Edited by Dorothy S. Severin. Madrid: Alianza Editorial, 1969 and reprints. Text similar to Cejador's, with some refinements. Introduction by Stephen Gilman.

2. Principal French Translations

*Celestine*. Translator unknown. Paris, 1527. Modern edition by Gérard J. Brault. *"Celestine": Critical Edition of the French Translation (1527)*. Detroit, 1963.

*La Celestine*, trans. Jacques de Lavardin (Paris, 1560?). Based on Italian translation of Ordóñez.

3. Principal Italian Translations

*Tragicommedia di Calisto e Melibea.* Venice, 1506. Translated by Alfonso de Ordóñez.

*Tragicommedia di Calisto e Melibea, . . . per Hieronymo Claricio.* Milan, 1514.

4. Principal English Translations

*The Spanish Bawd represented in Celestina.* Translated by James Mabbe. London, 1631. This translation has been reedited by James Fitzmaurice-Kelly, in Tudor Translations, VI (London, 1894); also, second series, II–V (London, 1925). An earlier draft of Mabbe's version is presented by Guadalupe Martínez Lacalle, *Celestine or the Tragicke-comedie of Calisto and Melibea* (London: Támesis Books, 1972).

Three abbreviated adaptations were also published in the sixteenth century; see Penney, *The Book Called Celestina* (below), p. 115.

5. Recent English Translations

*The Celestina.* Translated by L. B. Simpson. Berkeley: University of California Press, 1955. This is the sixteen-act *Comedia* only.

*Celestina.* Translated by Mack H. Singleton. Madison: University Press of Wisconsin, 1958.

*Celestina, or the Tragi-comedy of Calisto and Melibea.* Translated by Phyllis Hartnoll. London: Dent, 1959.

*The Spanish Bawd.* Translated by J. M. Cohen. Harmondsworth and Baltimore: Penguin Books, 1964.

6. Principal German Translation

*Ein hipsche tragedia.* Translated from Ordóñez's Italian version by Christoph Wirsung. Augsburg, 1520.

7. Principal Latin Translation

*Pornoboscodidascalus latinus.* Translated by Kaspar von Barth. Frankfurt, 1624.

SECONDARY SOURCES

The following are only a small fraction of the books and articles on *La Celestina.* I have chosen only influential or substantial works (restricted to books, in section 2). The Notes and References give some further titles. The reader who desires a more extensive list should consult *"La Celestina" Studies: A Thematic Survey and Bibliography 1824–1970*, by Adrienne Schizzano Mandel (Metuchen, N. J.: The Scarecrow Press, 1971). New contributions to the subject will, of course, appear in the standard bibliographies, such as *PMLA Annual Bibliography* (New York) and *The Year's Work in Modern Language Studies* (The Modern Humanities Research Association, Cambridge, England).

## 1. Bibliographical and Textual Problems

ADINOLFI, GIULIA. "La Celestina e la sua unità di composizione," *Filologia Romanza.* 1 (1954), 16–20. Argues for Rojas' authorship of all parts of *Celestina*; the textual complications are due to his contradictory desires—to achieve fame and to avoid public censure.

CRIADO DE VAL, MANUEL. *Indice verbal de "La Celestina."* Madrid: *Revista de Filología Española*, Anejo 64, 1955). By analyzing samples of different linguistic forms, Criado claims to show separate authorship for act I, but authorial unity for acts II–XXI.

HERRIOTT, JAMES HOMER. *Toward a Critical Edition of the "Celestina."* Madison: University of Wisconsin Press, 1964. An attempt to reconstruct the relationships of all the early editions, by collecting and studying all the variants.

NORTON, F. J. *Printing in Spain 1501–1520.* Cambridge, England: Cambridge University Press, 1966. Appendix B. Expert knowledge of the history of printing is applied to the early editions of *Celestina*; for the first time, all the Seville 1502 editions are shown to be false.

PENNEY, CLARA LOUISE. *The Book Called Celestina in the Library of the Hispanic Society of America.* New York: The Hispanic Society of America, 1954. A minute description of each copy owned by the library and a bibliographical survey of all editions, Spanish and other, up to 1600.

RIQUER, MARTIN DE. "Fernando de Rojas y el primer acto de *La Celestina.*" *Revista de Filología Española* 41 (1957), 373–95. Accepts the linguistic evidence of Criado del Val and others that Rojas was not the author of act I and finds reason to believe that he misread the anonymous manuscript in several places.

WHINNOM, KEITH. "The Relationship of the Early Editions of the *Celestina, Zeitschrift für Romanische Philologie* 82 (1966), 22–40. Criticizes Herriott for noting only variant readings and ignoring other valid evidence (e.g., woodcuts), and for obscuring the problem by not excluding texts which (in Whinnom's judgment) need not be considered.

## 2. Life of Rojas

CAREAGA, LUIS. "Investigaciones referentes a Fernando de Rojas." *Revista Hispánica Moderna* 4 (1937–38), 193–208. Interesting for its description of Rojas' burial place.

GILMAN, STEPHEN. *The Spain of Fernando de Rojas*. Princeton: Princeton University Press, 1973. The best and most complete attempt to re-create the life of Rojas (as far as the scanty documents permit) and the circumstances within which he and his converso family existed. Contains previously unpublished material.

SERRANO Y SANZ, MANUEL. "Noticias biográficas de Fernando de Rojas autor de *La Celestina*." *Revista de Archivos, Bibliotecas y Museos* 6 (1902), 245–99. Contains legal testimony from and about Rojas and his family.

VALLE LERSUNDI, FERNANDO DEL. "Documentos referentes a Fernando de Rojas." *Revista de Filología Española* 12 (1925), 385–96; 17 (1930), 183. More precious information concerning Rojas' life from the personal archives of a descendant.

————. "Testamento de Fernando de Rojas, autor de *La Celestina*." *Revista de Filología Española* 16 (1929), 366–88. The will and complete inventory of Rojas' personal effects, compiled at his death.

## 3. Literary Studies

BATAILLON, MARCEL. *"La Celestine" selon Fernando de Rojas*. Paris: Didier, 1961. The nature of act I, according to Bataillon, is comic; *Comedia* shifts the subject from a lover's folly to the destructive effects of passion; the "additions of 1502" attempt to redress the balance. The intention of the play is wholly didactic. Bataillon also examines *La Celestina* in its literary history. A lucid, finely argued book, the best exponent of the thesis that Rojas continues the tradition of the morality play into the field of secular entertainment.

BERNDT, ERNA RUTH. *Amor, Muerte y Fortuna en "La Celestina."* Madrid: Gredos, 1963. The author isolates each of these topics in *La Celestina* for separate discussion in relation to earlier medieval writers and to Rojas' contemporaries.

CASTRO, AMÉRICO. *"La Celestina" como contienda literaria.* Madrid: Taurus, 1965. Develops the author's familiar theses: the restless creativity of the conversos; the skepticism and corrosive criticism which lurks in their works under conventional moralizing; ethical conflicts, clashes of value are not resolved by Rojas, because the religious frame is lacking.

CASTRO GUISASOLA, F. *Observaciones sobre las fuentes literarias de "La Celestina."* Madrid: *Revista de Filología Española,* Anejo V, 1924. An early study of Rojas' literary sources, and still valuable.

CLARKE, DOROTHY CLOTELLE. *Allegory, Decalogue, and Deadly Sins in "La Celestina."* Berkeley: University of California Press, 1968. The author sees *La Celestina* as a composite of love allegory and moral allegory within which all Ten Commandments are transgressed and the Vices embodied in the characters' actions. Didacticism at its most extreme.

DEYERMOND, A. D. *The Petrarchan Sources of "La Celestina."* Oxford: The University Press, 1961. Starting from Rojas' quotations of Petrarch, Deyermond examines their importance and especially as concerns the ideas of fortune, death, and suffering in *La Celestina.* He finds Rojas' work anti-Petrarchan in its pessimism and lack of Stoic or Christian framework.

GILMAN, STEPHEN. *The Art of "La Celestina."* Madison: University of Wisconsin Press, 1956. Rojas has created a unique world in and by means of a dialogue which is both self-expression of the speaking "I" and search for the "other." Gilman brilliantly justifies Rojas' additions in the *Tragicomedia.* His existential view of the characters as "lives" presented in "dialogic situations" is questioned in chapter 5 above.

LIDA DE MALKIEL, MARÍA ROSA. *La Originalidad artística de "La Celestina."* Buenos Aires: Fondo de Cultura Económica, 1962. A minutely detailed and encompassing study of *La Celestina,* its dramatic antecedents and later imitations. The characters, situations, dramatic techniques—every formal aspect of the play is studied here. For Mrs. Malkiel, the unifying artistic vision was realism, in the service of a tragic sense of life. This is arguable, but the vast erudition, seriousness, and critical intelligence of this book make it indispensable.

MARAVALL, JUAN ANTONIO. *El mundo social de "La Celestina."* Madrid: Gredos, 1964. A brilliant historian looks at the crisis in the social world of Calisto and Melibea, the decline of the old nobility with its ideals of service, and the rising new aristocracy of money in pursuit of opulence and conspicuous consumption. *Celestina* is "the first document of man's struggle against alienation in modern history."

MARTIN, JUNE HALL. *Love's Fools: Aucassin, Troilus, Calisto and the Parody of the Courtly Lover.* London: Támesis Books, 1972. Places Calisto in the late medieval tradition of moralistic satire and parody of "courtly love."

MENÉNDEZ PELAYO, MARCELINO. *Orígenes de la novela,* III. 4 vols. Madrid: Nueva Biblioteca de Autores Españoles, 1905–1910. This is still an excellent survey of *La Celestina,* though outdated by recent discoveries in the area of bibliography. It is reprinted separately as *La Celestina* in "Coleccion Austral" (Madrid and Buenos Aires).

MORÓN ARROYO, CIRIACO. *Sentido y forma de "La Celestina."* Madrid: Ediciones Cátedra, 1974. Morón Arroyo's study did not appear until after I completed this book. He gives special emphasis to the religious and ideological background.

SEVERIN, DOROTHY. *Memory in "La Celestina."* London: Támesis Books, 1970. A study of the characters' recollections as part of their continuing experience.

# Index

189